YOU HAVE TO CHANGE

As a future BILLIONAIRE, the most important conversation with yourself: If you want to be a BILLIONAIRE, you have to change your habits and make it instantly happen. There is a luxury or there is the old pattern of your old habits. If you change your subconscious mindset, your habits start to shift. If your old habits change = Your LIFE changes. Take the first step. All human beings can achieve their goals. The main issue is, you are not a tree programed by the creator to be a tree. If you plant a tree it can only grow. The tree can never be a human being or an African lion. A bird can never be a tree. The horse can never be an African zebra. I really can say that you can change and re-program your mind into the mindset of a BILLIONAIRE. Our wrong pattern mindset has not been programed to think like a universal BILLIONAIRE. We have been programed to think like employees as someone who lives from paycheck to paycheck. The case is you have been born to be a BILLIONAIRE. If we go back to the animal kingdom: Why is an eagle called the king of the bird domain? Because he flies in an atmosphere where no ordinary bird can follow him. Why is the lion called the king of the animal kingdom? Because that big cat demands its respect. The African lion is not taller than an elephant; an African lion is not heavier than an elephant; the subconscious mind of a lion does not allow him to run away from a massive elephant. He vibrates subconsciously as the king of the animal kingdom. Warren Buffett, the second richest man, has been programed to vibrate subconsciously as one of the richest men the world has ever seen. He can´t be any other than to vibrate on the frequency of a BILLIONAIRE. He has been programed to be among the richest men on the planet. See, you must re-write a new program that changes your subconscious frequency into the mindset of a BILLIONAIRE. A mindset that demands billions of dollars. I was broke, I was young. I have earned very good money, but I had no idea what wealth was. I thought wealth = MILLIONAIRE. Then I understood, that wealth is in your DNA, a frequency that vibrates through money. I vibrated like an employee with good income on the frequency of my boss. It is very comfortable being an employee, but the reality is worse because you don´t benefit from that vibration. All you get is a little paycheck at the end of a month. When you change things around you, your frequency changes; if your frequency changes, you start to vibrate differently. A tree can only be a tree, but I can change from being a broke employee into an independent BILLIONAIRE.

How to redefine my future LIFE. As we emerge into a new world, the imagination of a better income sets a shining example.

I was impressed when I found out that my subconscious mindset dictates how I should live and run my future life. If your apartment is dirty and untidy, that is because of your subconscious mindset and your habitual beheaviour accepts the special situation. If you buy drugs and live daily on hamburgers, that is because your subconscious mindset has been programed to function like that. Just realize now that you have a new born child. That baby can only concentrate on being asleep or being awake to be fed. What I wanna say: The new born has not been programed yet, it must learn how it feels to be kissed; it must learn that hot water is painful. The moment the child learns the meaning of a hot flame, the child won´t grab into the flame again. It has nothing to do with a brilliant mind. The child learns by making mistakes, that is where the programing / lesson starts = through failure. It is painful to be rejected; it is painful not to be loved; it is painful not to have a family that supports you. The vibration of LOVE is important for children like oxygen. If the frequency of the essence of LOVE is not provided, the child can´t vibrate on behalf of LOVE. That child is going to send the frequency of a crazy vibration to the community where he / she grows up.

You want to bild wealth with the purpose of being free from the game of money

The world rewards actions and not potential

Someone gave me the book: Think and Grow Rich by the author Napoleon Hill. That book has changed my paradigm forever. Why? Because I have done exactly what the author urges me to do as a reader: I went to seminars. I have read the book more than one-hundred-fifty times and I still read it. Slowly my subconscious mind changed forever and imitates my book readings. I have learned how to live on the frequency of a pure wealthy man. The natural laws of the universe are so precise, that we don´t have difficulties building aeroplanes or even sending human beings to the moon. We can even time the landing to within a nano-second. I really can´t tell you how impossible it seemed back in those days, just to mention the idea: "We gonna fly to the moon..." -the case is: "If you can imagine landing on the moon = it is possible." I remember how impressed I was when I watched a movie about the history of aeroplanes. It took so much effort to keep the first plane for three seconds in the air. Their neighbours thought that these people who were trying to make an item fly were completely out of their mind in the sense of they should not waste their time on the idea of making people fly from - A - to - B- . Their dream was to fly into the air and across the ocean by plane. Doing mistakes was okay, but giving up was not an option. If they were willing to fight for the idea of flying across the ocean, why should I be afraid of stupid criticism? Forget about what the world teaches you. If it's in your fantasy, it is possible. The future is yours. Forget about the past it´s gone. Too many people waste their time living in the past, wishing they would had done this or that. The only thing that matters is your current LIFE situation and the future as a BILLIONAIRE. You   can´t waste your time in the past because your violent mother did not love you enough or the school teacher used to hate you. You are supposed to win in LIFE; you are supposed to have a rich LIFE full of abundance. Essentially, you are not on planet earth to function on a frequency of extreme negative vibrations, just because some idiots cannot dream.

Subconscious mindset

Your paradigm is a multitude of ideas within your subconscious mind. Someone put those pieces of information into your subconscious mind that is in control of your financial broke behaviour. Who is in charge of your broken behaviour? Yes, your environment: Schools, your parents, aunts, friends, your neighbour next door...etc... - knowledge is not necessarily power, taking action is the powerful force that guides to change the frequency of vibration. You change the frequency, your vibration changes, your subconscious mind gets re-programmed, your subconscious mind changes, your mindset knows how to become a BILLIONAIRE. Every BILLIONAIRE is surrounded by knowledge and books. Without books no wisdom for your subconscious mindset. A BILLIONAIRE collects as much knowledge as he can. Knowledge is only powerful if you put it into a tool for action. The knowledge must be properly organized and intellectually directed to aim for your financial target. Decide how you wanna live. You wanna waste your time? Do you prefer to live in the past full of regrets? Or do you wanna make the first step into a better future as a BILLIONAIRE? Don´t worry about what did not work in the past, you can´t delete your unique biographical history. The frequency is to make things immediately happen, that you have a chance to vibrate tomorrow, next week, next month, next year, from the fruits of your labor as a BILLIONAIRE. The school system has failed to teach you how to earn billions of dollars. Those teachers don´t know how to earn billions of money as an annual salary. They don't understand the frequency of a BILLIONAIRE.

Before you pick up your telephone, someone needs to dial your telephone number. If someone type in those digits at the frequency that matches your telephone number, it lets your telephone vibrate. If someone misdials your telephone number, your telephone can´t vibrate, right? Your telephone can only vibrate if the right numbers attract the vibration of your telephone. See, if your telephone operates on the vibration of frequencies, you must change your subconscious vibration to function on the frequency of a Billionaire. We can only attract what is in harmony with us. Your broken financial mindset matches the frequency of why you vibrate as a broken individual.

That broken harmony controls your subconscious LIFE in an untidy, dirty apartment. Success is one percent luck and ninety-nine percent replacing your old subconsciousness through a conscious mindset. Most idiots spend ninety-nine percent of their time on strategy and one percent on mindset. If being a BILLIONAIRE is all about replacing the mindset, you need then to study the mind more than anybody else by reading books written by BILLIONAIRES. Every BILLIONAIRE on planet earth has written a book. I studied the mind more than anyone alive. My desire to change my subconscious mind is still my number one goal. If you are really tired of the way you live your LIFE, if you really wanna take control of your LIFE...- take control of your subconscious mindset and change your paradigm. Confidence comes from knowledge. You are confident to drive a car because you have learned how to handle a vehicle. The image we hold of ourselves dictates the money we wanna earn, the relationship we wanna be in. Everyone has an idea of something we wanna do in LIFE. But the idea dies so fast as it comes into our minds. Everybody should win every single day. Does winning happen by accident or through preparations? Does a tennis player win all the time by accident or by preparations / training sessions? The focus must be to implement the idea with all aspects into your subconscious mindset. Two things you need to know if you wish to create wealth: Being rich is not wealth, a millionaire is not necessarily wealthy, wealth is your subconscious mindset, your subconscious mindset is your DNA = your unique fingerprint. Some people win the lottery; some people work hard and earn bigger money, but all of them waste the money instantly on items nobody needs to survive. Thus, they cannot save money to create wealth. If you do exactly what I say, you are likely to increase your income by more than one-hundred times. The mind is an activity and not a thing. Technically it is a living being, that needs to be nurtured with useful, inspiring ideas / positivity. We treat symptoms but not the cause of a broken mindset. The cause starts always in the none physical, which is your mind. The question is what is in your mind that makes you financially not a BILLIONAIRE?

The problem is, nobody can watch into your mind except the owner of the mind; underneath your conscious mind is your subconscious mindSET, which sets the standard for your current LIFE. The physical instrument that carries out the operation of your subconscious mindSET is your physical earthly body.

There is no limit to money or success in this world

The conscious broken mind is the natural thinking mind above the subconscious broken mindSET. That subconscious mindset sets the standard for your financial understanding. It accepts whatever you give it. It works like the earth. It does not care what you plant, but returns what you plant. You have the choice to plant the negative or the positive; it will both grow. The subconscious mind can´t determine what is real or what is toxic. If you plant negativity, it will affect your body's psyche in a toxic way. Pieces of information flow into your subconscious mind: News comes from the radio, from other people; from TV, from the press = most of it is absolute, nonsense. They tell you things that aren´t even true, but they keep telling you stupid pieces of information and you keep listening; we let them influence us. You are in charge of what is important to your subconscious mind; you are in charge of your subconscious mindSET. Set the record straight for your mind. You are in charge of creating your own economy, circumstances, and financial RESULTS. -you can reject all those information. Because if you don´t reject those pieces of information, it drops from your conscious mind into your subconscious mindset and affects your body. Why do we do that? Well, because we are programed to follow stupid, nonsense. That is what a paradigm is. How does a paradigm work?

When you are born your subconscious mind is wide open as the sky above you. Allow me to give you a very good example: If you are taken out of a Chinese-speaking home and put into a home that speaks Spanish, you grow up fluent in the Spanish tongue. If you are put out of a French home and set into a Polish home, you are going to learn to use the Polish language as a child very fluently. Thus, everything that is around you goes into your subconscious mind. We have an image in our minds that was formed when we were little infants. In the absence of clearly defined goals, we become strongly loyal to performing daily trivia, until we ultimately become enslaved by it. A paradigm is a program in our subconscious mind.

Superior knowledge + inferior results = causes confusion & frustration.

The point is, it is the subconscious mindset that produces RESULTS. -if you do not change the paradigm, nothing changes. The key to a new subconscious mind is, you must read and do exactly what a change requires.

Nothing changes by accident. Your subconscious mind dictates who you are. Your paradigm is a mental program that has exclusive control over our habitual behaviour. Look at the areas of your LIFE that your subconscious mind has enormous influence over. Your Paradigm controls your use of time. It is what you do with your mind.

Your paradigm controls your activity, your activity is your creativity, your creativity creates your effectiveness, your effectiveness controls your productivity, your paradigm controls your ability to earn billions of dollars. Most people are extras in their "own" movies. They say: Look at him / her; look at that man in China, and they make anyone else the star. If you wanna be the star in your own movie, you need to decide what you want in LIFE. Creativity is the opposite of routine, you must become very creative.

In times of rapid change, learners inherit the earth, while the learned find themselves beautifully equipped to deal with a world that no longer exists. The learners will inherit the earth - means, they never stop learning. Their journey is to expand their mind. Never change things by fighting the existing reality. To change something build a new model that makes the existing model obsolete.

You can change a new model of life because you can feel that it is possible.

Hang out with BILLIONAIRES long enough and it is just a matter of time until you become one of them.

There is no limit to how much you can earn with your mind.

A-B-C- of goals

A= Present RESULT = Conscious knowledge- old pattern- subconscious.
B = What I think I can do = plan
C = What I WANT = Fantasy

B = No inspiration so you return to -A-
A = Your subconscious comfort zone = you are stuck
C = Your fantasy does not ask how to get there you are just there

---

Fantasy ------ > Turn it into a theory = Am I able to do it? Remember people are able to fly to the moon. The dream started to go through failures.
Are you willing to accept failures and mistakes?

Fantasy ----- > Am I willing = theory

President Kenney asked Mister von Braun what it takes to land on the moon?
Mister von Braun: "The will to do it."

All you need is the will to do it. Know that you are going to get there.

The law of attraction and vibration.

Vaibration and attraction go together. Attraction is secondary law, vibration is a primary law. Everything vibrates, it is a law that everything moves. We live in an ocean of motion. A goal is a vibration a frequency to grow. If you can see it, it is possible to fly to the moon, you know your dream is not impossible. You are a lot more than you attract on the surface. You already have within....all that is required to attract whatever you WANT into your life. Everything is already here, everything is already in you.

Example: A bottle made of plastic. The bottle used to be oil and the water in it used to be gas. If you boil the water it goes back into the universe, if you burn the plastic it returns to the universe. The water and the water in your body is energy. Energy is vibration and vibration is frequency. We can put ourselves into the vibration to attract what we WANT. Our whole world operates on a frequency of vibration.

Conscious mind
Subconscious mind

Body

Your body is the instrument of your mind, your body steps into action, and produces RESULTS.

The body acts on behalf of the vibration it is in. But we also have a picture in mind, the bigger dream.

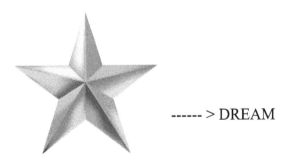

------ > DREAM

That dream is up on a different level it is an invisible world. Only one person can see it, that is you. The dream is responsible for every great advance of humankind.

The dream is invisible to the outside world. The dream to fly was invisible to those neighbours who saw them trying to keep the plane for only three seconds in the air; the dream to land on the moon used to be invisible to the outside world until it became reality. See, if you can dream it, it is possible to achieve it. How do we go from where we are to where we wanna be? The attraction starts within your invisible dream in the none physical world. This is a mind game, you must understand your mind if you really wanna make it happen. You control your vibration. Your brain is the electronic switching station. As you activate your brain cells, you alter the vibration you are in; as you alter the vibration, you alter what you attract into your LIFE. You must understand how to control the vibration.

Paradigm is a mind program. It´s a program in your mind that controls your behaviour. You already know how to do better than you are doing. But you are not doing it. Understand the part of your mind that knows things and the part that controls your behaviour.

Albert Einstein: Everything is energy, and that´s all there is to it. Match the frequency of your reality you WANT. And you cannot help but get that reality. It can't be any other way. This is not philosophy; this is physics.
-Match the frequency of the reality you WANT = Just get on the frequency of a BILLIONAIRE.

Example: A telephone number is a frequency to tune in on someone else´s frequency/telephone. If you dial the number / frequency the telephone with the right frequency starts to vibrate. You gonna ask, what does it have to do with my dream? See, your dream is a frequency that vibrates in your subconscious mind. Your dream is not yet a part of this world. If you have been stuck, if you have had a difficult time altering your income, if you have had a difficult time attracting into your LIFE the relationship or business that you WANT, it is because you are on the wrong frequency. And you are using the wrong tool.

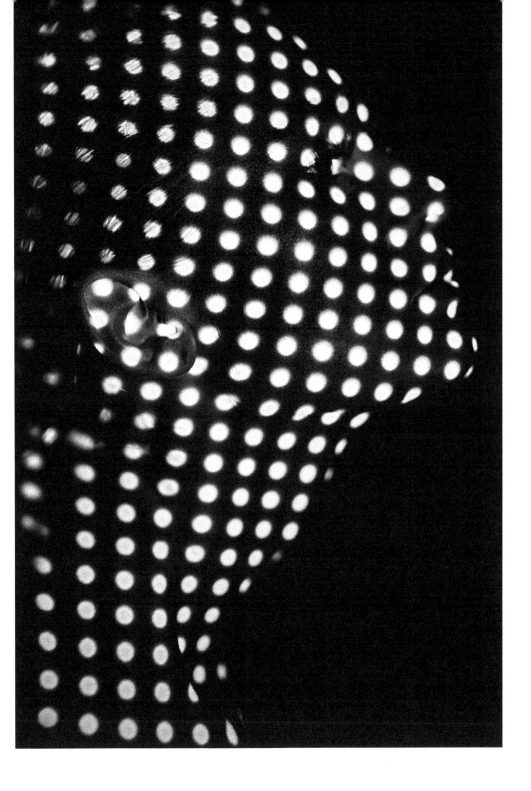

When you are onto a higher frequency, you are in a different world. The people you are still dealing with do not understand your shift into a better frequency. Because their frequency is different, they're gonna tell you: "You are crazy." Most BILLIONAIRES do not earn money in one place. They earn it exclusively through passive income. The wealthiest people do not work. You do not earn billions of money by working a nine-to-five job; that´s a false concept. You should embrace and love what you do. You should do the work for your inner satisfaction. The former King of Pop did not do the work just to earn money. He enjoyed creating and then performing his art. Michael Jordan did not work for the money; he worked for his inner frequency that vibrated through the scores on the basketball court. You cannot fire LeBron James from his work as a basketball player; he does the preparation behind the scenes because he programed himself to win everytime he enters the basketball court. He sets the frequency behind the scene, and thus, he is able to vibrate as the best player on the field.

Your spiritual DNA is perfect. It is the most perfect masterpiece the Lord (=Creator) has ever fashioned. There is a marvelous inner world within a man, and the revallation of such a world enables a man to do, to obtain and achieve anything he desirers within the bounds or limits of nature. Everywhere we go in nature we see perfect order. The body you are living in has been designed to function on principles according to nature. Your body is the perfect instrument to do what ever you wanna do in combination with your subconscious mind. The human body is a mass of energy; it´s a mass of molecules and high-speed vibration. And when the body does not vibrate with the principle of the law of our creator (= The Lord), it breaks down. By the time your body vibrates in harmony, it is alive and functions to its full capacity; it can automatically move to the right frequency to become a BILLIONAIRE. Your spiritual DNA is perfect; it requires no modification or improvement. The center of our consciousness is perfection; there is absolute perfection locked up within us, and that perfection is always seeking expression through perfection. With and through us there is something in us that wants to be expressed in a greater way. If you run - you wish to run faster. Whatever you do, there is something in you that wants to do better. Some people try a few times and then they fail and they choose to give up and quit.

The truth is, you have perfection locked up in you. Your spirit is 24 hours present, it never sleeps that´s why it is so powerful.

Unleash your inner beast. Nobody can obtain their ambitions until they learn to discipline their mental force and are able to control their thinking. You must learn to work with the law of the frequency that lets you vibrate as a BILLIONAIRE. It´s how you bring your mind into harmony with the law; it´s about letting off things of a lower nature, so that we can receive things of a higher nature.

The greatest in the world have spent years studying what they do; the greatest musicians have spent years perfecting their skills; the greatest have spent years training and perfecting their skills. There is no luck in winning repeatedly if you are a professional athlete. You're never gonna get higher things for nothing. You must sacrifice your time to study the world's greatest so that you can become greater. The whole universe functions on an equation of principles. The law applies to every person everywhere. Five apples plus five apples equals always ten apples.- that is a law. Get in harmony and study the law / equation of a BILLIONAIRE. If you understand that you have to work twice a day to understand the harmony of a law, what it takes to be a BILLIONAIRE, it becomes a habitual behavior. Everything we do is in control of our paradigm habits. A paradigm is a habit of good or strange behavior. If we WANT to change our LIFE so that we can become a BILLIONAIRE, we must understand that we ought to change our paradigm. It is crucially important to sacrifice the habit of our financial broke nature, for our higher BILLIONAIRE subconscious mindset. You gonna realize how important discipline is. It is a discipline that is constantly being chosen; you have to choose it. Nobody else can do it, or give it to you; it comes from deep within. You have to choose the pain of discipline; nobody else is going to do it for you; it comes from deep within. If you are not willing to sacrifice your old subconscious mindset to the mindset of a billionaire by reading books and taking actions, you probably won´t get financially better. If you WANT to lose weight, you must sacrifice your habit of eating to much food, if you don´t give it up you are never going to get a brilliant body shape or better health. Additionally, you must do a little bit of sport; going to the gym is a tool that lets your body vibrate, so that it stays in shape. Discipline yourself and start living in harmony with this new frequency that will let you vibrate into your new form of a body shape.

Working with the harmony of the laws is such a winning concept. You should be an aesthetic builder. Build a new financial wisdom, build an aesthetic financial frequency that vibrates into your bank account. If you don´t understand the laws, you will never be obedient to them. You are going to violate them. We have been programed not to live in harmony with the law of the universe. We are constantly violating the law to reach the level of a BILLIONAIRE. The word obey means to submit to rules or to follow orders or instructions. Obedience is the governor of all movements. A giant plane without its governor, would crah down to the ground, because it failed to obey its own laws to function as a plane. An intellectual giant who fails to follow the laws of learning will become the nature of an idiot. A student failing to follow or to obey the instructions of spirit, the law of The Lord (=Creator), will reverse the good and create evil; we are dependent entirly on obiedience for our billion dolloar success or failure in this LIFE.

A business has been founded on obedience; and each member obeys the laws of commerce to succeed. We must understand that we need to become obidient to the laws of a BILLIONAIRE if we wanna vibrate like a BILLIONAIRE.
Mother nature has not trouble in the world, she can´t solve; she has no burden. Why? All her operations are governed by the mighty law of harmony and order, which constantly removes every discord, which heals all diseases, and which supplies every need. Think of the health of your body, it could be better if you live in harmony with the laws.

You gotta be true to yourself, if you wanna be free, you must obey the laws. The more obedient you become, the more you gonna win. You must submit and understand the frequency of a BILLIONAIRE. Study the great BILLIONAIRES and model their frequency within your understanding of what it takes. Understanding only comes through studying. Dig into the program of a BILLIONAIRE.
Every BILLIONIARE serves a larger audience with very useful tools / equipments. If you wanna be a BILLIONAIRE learn to serve billions of people. If you serve them, the frequency of money that comes to you has been cretaed through your service. Your bank account starts to vibrate.

There is no secret becoming a BILLIONAIRE. You must create little things that serves ten billion people. If each of them pay you one dollar = you are worth ten billion dollars. Earning money is nothing but an equationalgame of frequency. A game consists of rules, if we talk about science we talk about laws. Being a BILLIONAIRE is an exact law. First law don´t waste money, second law follow law number one. That´s all there is = The law of cause and effect. The compamy founded by Steve Jobs, sends the frequency to attract and be in service for billions of people around the globe. The Apple company founded by the man who is in charge how we communicate in these days follows a law, that is the reason why the company is such in a great financial shape.

It takes three to five years to get rich as a millionaire but it´s a life pattern to RESULT forever as a BILLIONAIRE.

You have the possibility to shift the vibration you are in. You have to take that good energy and serve it to other people.

The **LAW** higher frequncy

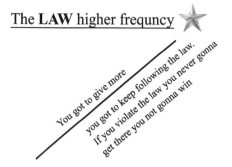

You got to give more
you got to keep following the law.
If you violate the law you never gonna
get there you not gonna win

Results right now - your current frequency

_____

_____

The laws of a billionaire are not man made by human beings, so they are never gonna be changed by human beings. The law of a BILLIONAIRE is a universal principle.

Example: Try to change the equation of six apples plus two apples equals eight apples. See, you can´t. Why? Because it is a law/ a universal principle. Go from vioating the law to live in harmony with the frequency of a very disciplined BILLIONAIRE. Step on the focus to provide better services. If you don´t study the vibration of a BILLIONAIRE you gonna stay in crises and ignorant as you are.

Stop blaming your parents, friends, etc...- quitt thinking backwards, think about it what comes next. How are you going to the next steps that is going to generate billions of money. Imagine you have sex with a beautiful woman. Do you keep your focus on the orgasm or do you enjoy the process of doing it? Don´t let your past dictate your future.

Three essential questions

1.) What has my LIFE been up to that point? Think about your current frequency. Is the vibration of your current bank account good or bad? You are the perfect creation by The Lord. Is your bank balance also the most perfect creation?

2.) What I wish my LIFE to be like

3.) Am I honest, and committed enough to make whatever changes my mindset to RESULT as a BILLIONAIRE?
- Start to move financially into the right direction
- Your RESULTS are a direct reflection of your current subconscious mindset.

You identify with your current RESULTS because it is in harmony with your subconscius mindset. Napoleon Hill studied five hundred millionaires, put his notes on paper, and formed a book called: Think and Grow Rich. That is exactly what you must do. Learn and study at least five-hundred BILLIONAIRES and understand why they are among the wealthiest people on planet earth. Then you gonna realise, it did not happen by accident. Become the master of your current LIFE and step higher to master the frequency that let you vibrate as a BILLIONAIRE. Once I understood that I am in charge of my vibration I began immediately to seperate myself from my old consciousness that keeps me forever broke. The big change starts within your home with a clean tidy apartment, the man in the mirror is in charge to clean the apartment. I changed the direction of my apartment by setting everything on the frequency to be clean and tidy.
How many resources of income did I had? All I had was my job
(JOB = Just Over Broke).
I started to provide services across the world. The frequency was so brilliant that I attracted followers.
Thoughts become things by taking actions. My apartment became a clean thing by taking actions. I lost weight by taking actions. The thing called my physical human body is in very good shape. If your physical human body vibrates your are on the frequency of sport to loose weight. If your body does not vibrate you gain weight. If your mind does not vibrate you gain weight. If your mind does not vibrate

on the frequency of a BILLIONAIRE , money can´t find its way to your bank account. A BILLIONAIRE wakes up at least at five o´clock morning time or a little bit earlier. He pays attention to money by being an early bird. Because these people understand that if you don't wake up early, someone else is going to make the profit. All of them listen to the latest news around the globe. Business is war, you ought to be prepared. There is no substitute for hard work.

More is more
More books = MORE
More wisdom = MORE
More money = MORE
More billions = MORE
More sex = MORE

The more you study, the more you read, the more you do sport = Always more = The more you can win.

Submit to solve more fundamental problems and not symptoms. The fundamental problem is that you only have a job as your income and not a product that serves billions of people. Create products. What are the problems of the world that needs your service? Education, water, health care are the fundamental needs of the world ...- if you can solve any of those problems you gonna end up automatically as a BILLIONAIRE. Make the committment to submit to the frequency of a BILLIONAIRE. First comes the idea to submit to solve the problems of human beings, if you handle a problem the world pays you. Don´t look at the glass as half full or half empty. Keep the focus on the next step. Focus on tommorow.

What to say: Many of us are pretty comfortable in their LIFE. We got our little job. We signed a contract with a company, but in reality we don´t like waking up to work for our BOSS. As a normal thinking person you confirms not to change your current situation because it requirers work and work is not comfortable. The comfort zone of being an employee pays your morgage, pays for your food and a little bit for your car. Employees are just coating along taking the line of least resistance, you just wanna get by. Of course it is a very common understandbale attitude. The problem is...

The comfort zone: Once we stop reading, stretching, seeking and risking, we stop growing into a point of a higher better vibration. The comfort zone frame of mind is settling for what we are today. The danger of a comfort zone is that it does not hurt and it might even feel good; you think it is a good place to be. It holds you back from growing on the frequency of a BILLIONAIRE. You're not gonna accomplish anything in your current results / comfortzone. If you say you like it as it is, you do disintegrate. If a person says: "I like it as it is you advertising ignorance. The question should be can I entertain a new idea today, tommorrow, next week, next month, next year..etc? Every idea that is positive, creative, constructive, is worth following it, if it improves the quality of your LIFE. You are born with all tools to improve your LIFE and physical body. You are born rich. Only if you understand the power of frequency then you are able to understand your LIFE. If you don't RESULT the way you imagine, the truth is your way does not work. You must change people around you, you must change the frequency. If you are overweight and you can't get the RESULT of a better body shape, you must change the frequency that let's your body vibrate that you can loose weight.

Do exactly what I tell you to do and vibrate with this book, at least by reading it one-hundred times. Remember, your way does not work. What works is my way.Try instantly my way. I want you to take this book seriously, because it can bring you on the frequency to change your current RESULTS into the atmosphere of a BILLIONAIRE. Decide what you want. You want a change or do you want your current RESULTS? You must have the will to make it happen if you wanna make it as a BILLIONAIRE.

Don't listen to your parents if you have a vision, or your so-called friends or neighbours. Do they pay your bills? Thus, what do you need their opinion for? Their opinion is a frequency to keep you financially broke-minded. Find out what you like and what you need in LIFE. When I started I said to myself: "I can't live like this anymore. I must have my own boeing 747 plane, my own island and of course my own business. At the same time I needed to admit how much I love people / human beings. I enjoy to give and serve. I wanna see a smile on a face.

Knowing and doing are not the same. Reading and memorizing are not going to make you successful.

What turns you into a BILLIONAIRE is the understanding and application of wise thoughts that counts. You must create, go out and act on behalf of the law that transfroms you into a BILLIONAIRE. You must bust out of the shell and do exactly what is reqired to become a BILLIONAIRE. Deep inside of your special subconscious mind is a dream hidden. That dream should become a reality, if you put your focus exclusively on it. You are not on planet earth to just pay bills, you hve been born to have a rich LIFE full of abundance as a BILLIONAIRE on planet earth.

Vernon Howard said: "You can´t escape prison if you don´t know you are in a prison cell. That dream you got that comes to your mind, I suggest you look at it as your purpose to full fill. Just do it. Don´t wait start immediately whether you feel prepared or not. Say to yourself: "I am going to get it, I am going to make my LIFE a billion dollar success by using the law of frequency that is going to send billions of dollars to my bank account. The only thing that can flow into your LIFE is based on what is circulating / flowing around your LIFE. If you watch only trash TV = your subconscious mind is going to build a LIFE full of trash and none sense. If you read and re-read books written by BILLIONAIRES your subconscious mind is going to vibrate automatically on the frequency on behalf of those books you have been reading. If you use all information aquired from all books written by BILLIONAIRES and take them to action and action again / repetition again, if you do it long enough you can only get the RESUTS of a BILLIONAIRE. Order is the first law of creation and the second order is movement. Guess what is going to happen if you have order and movement, what happens in LIFE there is a pattern of growth that is going to develop. The order is to make the decision no matter where I am, no matter how well I am doing, I can do much better. A movement is a system of orders. Being a BILLIONAIRE is first a system of orders / laws / rules that a subconscious mindset needs to follow. A clear understanding where the journey begins is actively taking actions towards to shift the paradigm. The author who wrote the book - Think And Grow Rich said: "You must know why you WANT it, where you WANT it, when you WANT it and when exactly you WANT it and how you gonna get it. So we need check points to help us stay on course.

A frequency is energy and energy is timeless. Success is a journey to aim for a destination. Success has always been called a journey; it is not something you get or become; it is timeless and endless because it is a frequency. Being excellent means the commitment to completion. The steps to get there might be challenging, but understanding the steps is easy. The committement to completion is to step on the frequency of a BILLIONAIRE that makes you vibrate forever as a BILLIONAIRE. It means completing things around your home; it means completing things at your work; it means completing the things in your personal LIFE. It is a commitment to step up the frequency of a Billionaire for completion as a BILLIONAIRE. Be completely honest with your own story regarding recognizing where you presently are in LIFE. The mental adjustment must be made to let you vibrate at the frequency of a BILLIONAIRE. Look at it as your first investment, if you step on the frequency of a BILLIONAIRE. Before you step on the frequency of a BILLIONAIRE, text down where you see potential to support people. How do you wanna serve / support billions of people. Why should they pay you? Promise to yourself that you step on the frequency immediately and do everything necessary to inspire people. If the world wants your product, your bank account is going to vibrate financially.

Bruce Lee said: "You have to become the water in the glass."

For a marvelous mindset, use this book daily until your BILLIONAIRE mindset has been set in order. If your subconscious mindset is in harmony with the core essence laws of a BILLIONAIRE, it becomes habitual behaviour. Make sure the people you are surrounded with are extremely successful.
The environment is very important. The difference between none achievers and real achievers seems not to raise so much from nature as from habit, custom, and education. Most people live morally, physically and intellectually in a very restricted circle of their potential beings. We make very little use to change the subconscious mind. Somewhere in our subconscious mind lies sleeping the seed of being a BILLIOANIRE. Everything is already there to achieve your billion dollar dream; it is just a matter of learning how to use your subconscious mind.

As the energy of the subconscious mind changes, the vibration of the body changes. Think about for a moment of a glass of water. What happens if you hit the glass of water with a little spoon? The glass and the water starts to vibrate. The glass vibrates and you hear a fine tune noise. The sound is a vibration and the spoon is the tool that inspirers the glass to vibrate, because the glass vibrates, the water in it vibrates. If energy vibrates your phiscal state of being goes somewhere. You have to go to your subconscious faculties and develope a frequency to vibrate like a BILLIONAIRE. Change your vibration: READ BOOKS + REMEMBER + REPEAT = RESULTS OF A BILLIONARE.

If you do it very well, you just can´t help to work and vibrate like a BILLIONAIRE. Learning is if you step constantly on the frequency and entertain your subconscious mind to become a BILLIONAIRE. The aim of a BILLIONARE is RESULTS. If the RESULTS are not there you have no one to blame because you are not on the frequency of a BILLIONAIRE. You vibrate on another frequency if the RESULTS are not there. A top CEO reads over one-hundred books per year. The average person reads one book a year.

Every future BILLIONAIRE is requested to read those books

1. Life is a snowball - by warren Buffett
2. Value Investing - by Benjamin Graham
3. Rule Number One - by Phil Town
4. Alwaleed - by Riz Khan
5. Business at speed of thoughts - by Bill Gates

6. Direct from Dell - by Michael Dell
7. Made in America - by Sam Walton
8. Call me Ted - by Ted Turner
9. Principles - by Ray Dalio
10. Staying ahead of the game - by George Soros

11. The Virgin way - by Richard Branson

12. The black swan - by Nassim Taleb

13. How to be rich - by J. Paul Getty

14. What it takes - lessons in the pursuit of excellence - by Stephen A. Schwarzmann

15. Shoe dog - A memoir by the creator of NIKE

16. How to win at the sport of business: If I can do it you can do it - by Mark Cuban

17. Zero to one - by Peter Thiel

18. Onward: How starbucks fought for his life - by Howard Schultz

20. Bloomberg - by Mike Bloomberg

21. Sterring clear: How to avoid dept crisis and secure our economic future - by Peter G. Peterson

22. Only the paranoid survive: How to identify and exploit the crises

23. The Alchemy of financeby George Soros

24. Invest like a billionaire - by George Soros

25. Think and grow rich - by Napoleon Hill

26. Too big to fail - by Andrew Ross Srkin

27. The physics of wallstreet - by James Owen Weatherall

28. The Wolf of Wallstreet by Jordan Belfort

29. Confession of a Wallstreet analyst - by Dan Reingold

30. More money than God - by Sebastian Mallby

How you live your LIFE vs. how you wish to lead your LIFE. You need confidence to be an authentic BILLIONAIRE. If you read this book and do exactly what I suggest, you can't help, but only succeed as a BILLIONAIRE. What happens in the future is the decision you make today. I am a professional BILLIONAIRE and still do exactly what I am supposed to do as a BILLIONAIRE. My LIFE changed so much, I made a decison on one thing: "From now on I gonna repeat what I have learned and keep repeating it until I am the richest BILLIONAIRE that have ever walked the earth. I said I gonna serve people world wide and I will continue to serve people worldwide. Growth is an enormous part of LIFE. If something is not growing, it dies. If we are going to grow, there is one thing that must be done: We are going to change automatically. We can't stay where we are and get better RESULTS. It just does not work. You change your paradigm; you change your LIFE. All you want in LIFE is your health and the will to earn bigger money. Two things you must know, if you want to create wealth. We have to know your current RESULTS and you have to know where you wanna go; and then you must step on the journey of a BILLIONAIRE through readings and actions. Massive actions take you into the direction of a BILLIONAIRE.

You keep getting the same RESULTS over and over again because you don't repeat what you learn, if you don't repeat, you are not on the frequency of a BILLIONAIRE. The information of YOUR mindset does not drop into YOUR subconscious mind as a program. Learn to control the flow of thoughts. Thoughts is energy, let it flow into YOU and through YOU, improve it, repeat everything you learned, and everything gets connected. See, if you repeat to read a book again, there is a familiar energy flowing through you again a frequency of a feeling that lets your subconscious mind vibrate. If your subconscious mind vibrates through repetition, you feel automatically good because of the positive energy you vibrate on. If you repeat to read a book again, your mental programm / paradigm steps into an habitual behaeviour, that habit is going to dictate if you are going to vibrate on behalf of the law of a BILLIONAIRE. Almost - most beheaviour is habitual. A paradigm is a "BLACK & WHITE" thing. It does not matter how hard you work or how many hours you in **...IF THE PARADIGM DOES NOT CHANGE, THE RESULTS ARE GOING TO REMAIN THE SAME TODAY, TOMMOROW, NEXT WEEK, NEXT MONTH, NEXT YEAR...ETC.**

I want you to burn this into your mind: "When your paradigm stays in control NOTHING CHANGES. You can try as hard as you want, if the paradigm remains in control, you never going to become a BILLIONAIRE. We must ask ourselves: **How do we control the flow?**

How do we control the flow of thoughts and energy?
How do we let it flow freely through us?

Well, we got the ability to choose based on the fact that, our mental faculties are the best. What is a paradigm shift? It means shifting your mental program that allows you to function and work on the frequency of BILLIONAIRE. If you are on the frequency of a BILLIONAIRE, you are going to subconsciously think, act, talk and vibrate like a BILLIONAIRE who is able to generate billions of dollars. The first thing to do is the constant repetition that is essentially the opposite of your current mental program / paradigm. Through constant, consistent repetition, the information how to become a BILLIONAIRE drops into your subconscious mind. That´s when it becomes a habitual behavior. Second the personal experience of an impact.

Why repetition is necessary when changing paradigms.

Example: If you read a book, you focus on the next word, the next sentence, the next page, the next chapter. The more you re-read / repeat a book the more comfortable you are to make it through the book, the more comfortable your are with the same book - the more you explore what is written between those lines of a book, you are then able to grab the essence, what defines the book, if you repeat it at least one-hundred times, it drops automatically into your subconscious mind, your subconscious mind sets the MINDSET, your habitual beheaviour = THE REAL YOU = BILLIONAIRE.
Repetition changes your broken habit into the mindset of a BILLIONAIRE. Through repetition everything in LIFE changes. Positivity attracts positivity, negativity can only attract negativity if you repeat negative things. That is a universal law. You repeat the positive frequency of a BILLIONAIRE, your subconscious mindset can´t help to vibrate on behalf of a BILLIONAIRE.

Example: How do you know your name is your name? You know your name because your parents did the repetition over and over and over again, until it droped into your subconsciousness and you became used to it. When someone asks for your name, it became an automatic habit to mention you go by the name: XYZ (...whatever your name is...).

The law of attraction if the vibration of your subconscious mindset. Your subconscious mindset is the purpose and the reason for living. All we can do since we were infants is to act, talk and model after the people around us. First you learn how to talk like your mother and father, then you go to school, that is a social system, you wish to fit into this environment, you better learn how to act and talk in the colorful manner of the school environment, if you wish to fit in order to experience a group accepting. If you do match the frequency of the environment, you are accepted as a member. It is crucially important to surround yourself with successful people, if you do, you learn the techniques that make them BILLIONAIRE - you learn their language and understand the frequency why they vibrate as successful people. Ninety-five percent of all people live their entire LIFE the way they don't want to live. You better start thinking for yourself and improving, instead of following stupid people - that's why the book is called: THINK AND GROW RICH. You must be confident to make a lot of failures. Don't think the journey to become a great BILLIONAIRE, is a journey without failure. The case is, if you wanna grow, you must step out of the box of your current financial RESULTS.

It is reported that Thomas Edison tried three-thousand times, before he had the idea, how a light bulp should work. He did not say: "I failed three-thousand times". He mentioned that there were three-thousand steps to how a light bulb could not work. Well, there are different steps until you learn and understand how things work to serve its purpose. The light bulp is a tool and in that tool / in that bulb or glass is a wirer, if someone switches the light on by pressing the button on the wall - in a room, the electronical frequency sets the wirer in vibration, through vibration light appears. Thomas Edison needed to study and re-study and re-study; it took him three-thousand times until he could understand the frequency, how a light bulp must vibrate until the wirer gives light. See, Thomas Edison did not give up after trying three or four times; he kept believing in his dream ⭐ and took the steps to make it happen. Winning and losing is only a matter of how hard and often you try to win. Mister Edison could see his vision in his mind. He had no idea how to get there. All he needed to do is to fail three-thousand times until he vibrated on the knowledge of how a light bulb should shine. They say: "If it is in your mind / fantasy it is possible to bring it into the physical world. You must accept failure as an option to get better. If you make progress with each step through failure, you are a winner.

You can´t win the battle against the whole world if you can´t win the war against the frequency of your own mind. Imagine if Thomas Edison would have asked his neighbor, mother, father, so-called best friends; all of them would have recommended him to give up trying. If he had given up, what would the world look like without light bulbs these days.
Freedom means living your LIFE the way you want to live your LIFE. And not how a society of broke people wants you to structure your LIFE. You have the ability to choose to win by keeping trying or to lose by giving up.

Don't let circumsatance control you. As a professional BILLIONAIRE you control what goes into your subconscious mind that dictates your paradigm.

We human beings are the only creatures on the planet that´s totally disoriented in our enviroment in pursue of our purpose.

The birds are not confused because they have been fashioned to fly, the fish in the water are not confused - because they have been fashioned to swim. All animals are in harmony with their enviroment. Only human beings are confused and disoriented in their own enviroemnt on planet earth. We have been given by The Lord (=Creator) our won mental faculties / free will to create our own enviorment. We human beings have higher faculties and the average person has no knowledge of how to operate with them or how to develope them. The case is we have been trained to be controlled by what is going on around us. We are raised to be ignorant and not conscious. There is actually a small percentage of the population that have a clear understanding of what they are capeable of doing. Only a little minority of conscious people act on the frequency of being conscious. Two percent of the people think, three percent think that they do think and ninety-five percent rather consider to die than to think. If you watch what most people are doing, it is very obvious these idiots are not thinking.

We are here on planet earth to do the work as a creator. It´s the thinking that controls you not the age. You have to use your age as an advantage. As long you are not dead you have the advantage to set the frequency to vibrate into the LIFE you wish to live.

The cause of fear is ignorance, ignorance out in a conscious LEVEL as doubt and worry. You either doubt or you worry. Then we take whatever image comes into our consciousness of the doubt and worry and we turn it over to our emotional mind that what causes the fear. That fear has then to be expressed through the body. The body is an instrument. If fear is negative energy it can only get through your body, it sets up the vibration known as anxiety.

Anxiety is not expressed, anxiety becomes suppressed and the supression turns into depression, which turns into disease, which turns to decay.

Fear is a negative track:

1: Ignornce

2: Don´t worry

3: Fear

4: Anxiety

5: Suppression

6: Depression

7: Diseas

8: Disintergration

The opposite of all that is knowledge and wisdom. There is only one way to get knowledge and that is to study and re-study again and again. Unfrotunately, school does not serve its purpose; school should teach to LOVE to study because study leads to the opposite of "don´t worry". The opposite of "don´t worry" is understanding. Study deletes the fear of depression: Through study we understand where the fear starts. This understanding makes us understand that the whole universe operates by laws. One of the laws is the law of opposite, the opposite of "don't worry" is understanding. The "don´t worry" leads to fear, understanding leads to faith, the faith leads to expression. The Expression is not depression, it´s not suppression, it´s not anxiety, the faith leads to well being, the well being is expression and acceleration because we are at ease, we are not disease.

And when we understand that our world starts to change, it´s by understanding that we learn how to deal with these negative tracks:

1: Ignorance

2: Dont worry

3: Fear

4: Anxiety

5: Suppression

6: Depression

7: Disease

8: Disintergration

Fear is also doubt. The doubt becomes the cause of the fear, which is the cause of anxiety; fear is the effect / vibration .What is the opposite of the doubt? Study and understanding. If you want to find out who you really are, aof course, you need to study to delete the lack of understanding. If you keep studying, you gain a better understanding. If it´s you you are doubting, that means you don´t understand yourself well enough. You must get a better image of yourself; you must get a true image of yourself; understand who you are and how you function as an individual, realizing the physical body you are living in is an instrument given by The Lord (=Creator). Your body is the instrument of your subconscious mind. And the subconscious mind / THE REAL YOU expresses itself with & through the thing we call our physical body on earth. The invisible power to achieve whatever you want has been already implemented into you. All you need to do is step on the frequency and release it by re-programming your subconscious mindset.

The higher spiritual side is your intellectual side. Your intellectual factors run through your earlier perceptions.

1: Reasoned

2: Imagination

3: Memory

4: Intuition

We are spiritual human beings and that´s where greatness is hidden. Greatness is hidden in understanding the spiritual essence of who we are. Our spiritual DNA is perfectly fashioned by The Lord. It requires no improvement, and that essential perfection is deeply hidden in us. The trick is figuring out how to express it in a greater / bigger way. The only thing that can oppress your expression is not your mother, father, your environment; only the man in the mirror can express himself. If you have difficulties with your parents or friends, change your friends. You must be strong, be strong enough to follow your dream.

Martin Luther King said: "I have a dream." He never said: " I have a plan or a bank account." He had an image in his brilliant mind. He was a spiritual being, an African-American who spoke the language of The Lord, the frequency of LOVE. That HEAVENLY frequency vibrates and touches people all over the world. That´s why his speech to this day is timeless . The frequency and the vibration of LOVE does not age. His speech was the universal language of the Lord (= Creator), which is the essence of LOVE.

What problems to solve if you wanna be a Billionaire

1: Create cancer healing programm

2: Invent a pill to destroy HIV

3: Education an institute that prepares student to reach their true potential

4: Bio printing / Organ printing

5: Clean water supply

6: AI - Artificail intelligent

7: Free Wifi for everybody

Being a BILLIONAIRE is not a dream or something you hope to find. It only comes with being obsessed; it comes when you constantly work on it like you breathe oxygen, constantly thinking about it, constantly making sacrifices; you become a BILLIONAIRE by dedication = dedicating your LIFE and business to being the very best on the planet.

The average CEO works sixty-five hours a week. A future BILLIONAIRE does not mind working during the weekend or when he goes on holiday. Because they don't work for the weekend. A BILLIONAIRE builds something they LOVE. You must find something that lets you vibrate, if you vibrate that´s good for you because you LOVE it. The vibration is the frequency of an inspiration that excites you. The vibration lets you pursue your dream with everything you have. You don´t doubt yourself; you do not hold yourself back, and you don´t assume you are gonna fail as a BILLIONAIRE.

Billionaire Mark Cuban said: "Having an exit strategy means you are not fully committed to your success as a future BILLIONAIRE."

Many BILLIONAIRES tried to copy their role models; it makes sense, you want to follow in the footsteps of other people who inspirered you. But you can´t spend your whole career copying other people, you must go out on your own. That`s why several BILLIONAIRES attribute their success not to their wallets, but to their subconscious minds.

A billionaire's success begins with innovations. Each BILLIONAIRE saw a gap in the world, something people were missing, a need that was not being satisfied, and they turned that observation into an idea, a product, and then into a business. But what does it mean to try something new? Innovation does not always mean building something new from the ground up. Many of the world most succesful inventions already existed.

Being a BILLIONAIRE means to be the absolute best on the planet. Build a monopoly such as APPLE , WhatsApp, Microsoft, Twitter, Tesla, Coca Cola.

They tried very hard to compete with them.

Pepsi is not Coca Cola;
Samsung is not iPhone
Toyota is not Harley Davidson

However, if you build your way up, you have a chance to monopolize at least a niche in any other industry.

"The good LIFE is expansive. There is another way to live life that does not cost as much, but it isn't any good." -A lot of it reflects the truth in this sentence.

How to turn your annual income into a monthly income?

First, you must qualify by attracting good money by being good and very professional. A professional athlete gets paid like Kobe Bryant or LeBron James if he works his skills and qualifies for it each season.
Money has to be earned and there is a law for it. Like there is a law that governs the whole universe. The law of competition is exactly how you should program your subconscious mindset. If you set your subconscious mindset to function on the frequency to earn billions, you can't help but to earn billions. If you set your subconscious mindset to work a nine-to-five job you can only earn what has been agreed in your working contract.

The amount of money your earn will be in exact ratio to these three points:

1: The **NEED** what you do

2: Your ability to do it

3: The **DIFFICULTY** there will be in repalcing you

1: The **NEED** for what you do is already there = *The Lord (= Creator) gave you a purpose.*

2: The ability to do it

3: The **DIFFICULTY** there will be replacing you = *It will be taking care of if you take care of point number two*

Focus only on one point = that is number two

It means whatever you do you wanna get better at it. Just keep working and keep getting better at it.

There isn´t any competiton, the only competitor is the man in the mirror and the man in the mirror is the frequency of your reflexion.

You can´t fix the world until you fix your own subconscious mindset.

There are only three strategies for earning BILLIONS

M 3 = 1% use this strategy. This group earns all the money. 99% of all the money that is earned goes to a very small selected group of people. These people multiply their time by setting up multiple sources of income.

M 2 = 3% use this strategy. It's where you invest to earn money. If you invest you must know what you do, if you wanna earn money by investing.

M 1 = 96% use this strategy and it won't work and it has never worked =

$$\frac{\text{Time}}{\text{Money}} = \text{You} \quad \text{trade your valuable time on planet earth for money.}$$

- Trading time for mone is a strategy that has inherent problems. You can't become a BILLIONARE.

M 3 = How do you set up multiple sources of income? Some people would think to apply for a second job. The truth is you can set up multiple sources of income where you earn money while you are sleeping. It has never been easier than in these days.

You can turn your annual income into a

MONTHLY INCOME

This can be accomplished by having ...

MULTIPLE
SOURCES OF
INCOME

All wealthy people have always had...

MUTIPLE
SOURCES OF
INCOME

Money makes you what you already are. If you are not a nice person , more money makes you a terrible person. If you are a nice person, you become, through money, a nicer rich individual. Money is a magnifier.

When someone says money is not important, that is absurd. Money is a very important tool.

Connect the dots
- Earn money
- Enjoy Freedom
&
Begin to live the LIFE, you were designed to live. Creating money does not happen by accident, if you don´t gain an awareness of what and who you make you tick, you never gonna be free and a BILLIONAIRE.

Most people live in a cage and they don´t even know they are in prison. See, you are the highest creation fashioned by The Lord himself. There is nothing on planet earth that is called: The perfect masterpiece by The Lord. The case is, we humans are completely disoriented in our environment. All the other creatures are completely at home in their enviroement. We have been given the mental faculties to create our own enviorement. School does not teach us how to become a BILLIONAIRE.

The world treats you how you treat yourself.

Your cell phone has its own frequency, if I wanna reach you I must dial your telephone number / your frequency.
If I dial the wrong number I can't get on the frequency of your telephone = we can´t talk. I have to match the right frequency so that we can have a conversation via telephone.

Thought is the frequency of energy. Thought waves are cosmic energy that vibrates deep within your sub-conscious mindset. Everything you wish to be is already in you. Every great leader that has ever lived is in agreement that you can become whatever you think is alright for you. But most people spend time thinking about what they don't want. They spend time thinking: "I am so sick living this way. I am so tired of never being able to take a nice vaccation. Those people attract and send negative vibrations. They magnetize themsleves what they don´t want.

It we think of the telephone, your sub-conscious mind works exactly is like a telephone.

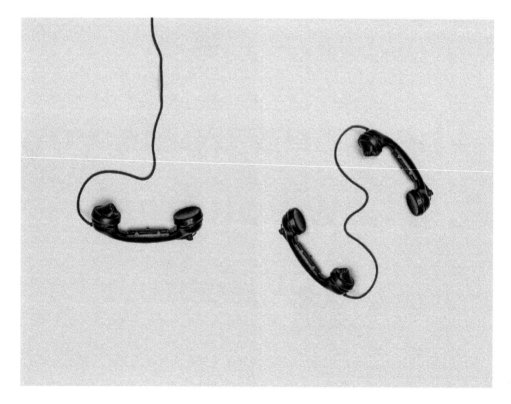

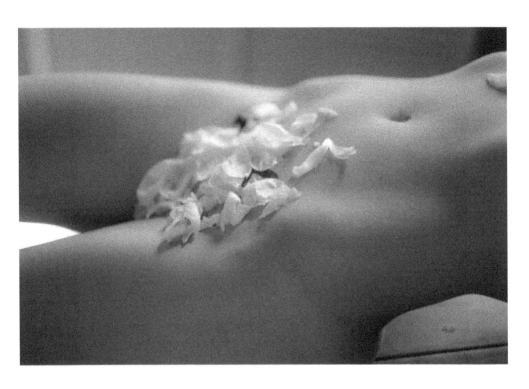

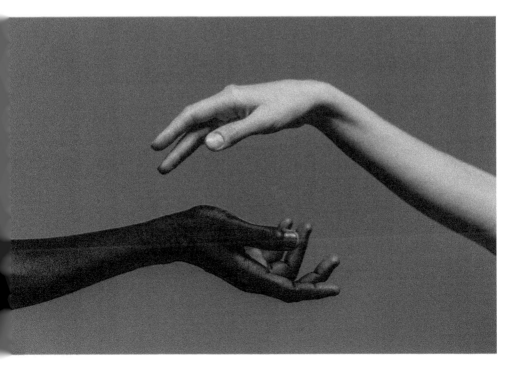

When you get on another person's frequency by dialing his telephone, you are one with them and magic starts to happen. Someone can be in Moscow while you are in Sidney. All that happens through frequency.

Everything we want in LIFE is already here, but we must step on the frequency to get it. We must get in tune with it so that we can vibrate as BILLIONAIRES. And if we do it, magic happens.
The frequency to become a BILLIONAIRE is already there; all you need to do is to tune in and dial the right number to become a BILLIONAIRE.

How to get the right number? By asking for the right number ?
How to ask for the right number? Get in touch with a BILLIONAIRE like you try to get in touch with a beautiful woman.
How? Every BILLIONAIRE has written a book - buy books written by BILLIONAIRES.
If you read books written by BILLIONAIRES, your subconscious mind starts to vibrate like a BILLIONAIRE.
As we activate brain cells, everything in us starts to change. See, if you step on the frequency of a BILLIONAIRE, the magic of your subconscious mindset starts to happen. You vibrate and have the ability to become a BILLIONAIRE.

Everything in LIFE has its own frequency. You want a descent feminine woman? Step on her frequency and let her vibrate in her feminine energy. Become one with the frequency you want. You can have everything you want in LIFE if you understand the universal law of frequency and vibration. If you want to know the telephone number of a beautiful woman, you need to ask her. And if you dial her telephone number, her telephone vibrates.
If you know the cell phone frequency of the president of the USA, you can let his phone vibrate. Find out what the frequency is.

Wo are we, if not the impact we have on others.

Look at your present RESULTS.

Right now you can only attract what you are in harmony with.

You are talking about healt issues? Take a look at the shape of your body.
You your not on the frequency to have a slim body shape? It means you are
in harmoney with your body.
You have a loud mouth wife in your LIFE, that´s exactly what you attracted.
Nobody has given her to you.
If you don´t like things you can change it.

Energy attracts good or bad energy.

Whatever we are thinking controls the vibration we are in. As we think we are
activaiting brain cells that causes the vibrations in our body. To move your
arm up and down you have to activiate brain cells to do that. What you think
dictates how you feel. Feeling is the language of subconsciouness. When
you talk about how you feel, your feelings are the vibration you are in. If you
feel terrible, you are in a terrible vibration. Change your thinking. Most people
in a terrible vibration doesn´t wanna hear that.

---------------------- Frequency--

Make a descision to become one ....
..with what you

WANT

You can create your own economy, own LIFE, own LOVE - LIFE.
The truth is we are already doing it = your current financial broken LIFE has
been created by you. You attracted your broken financial LIFE; you also
attracted your LOVE LIFE, you are in. The real you, your subconscious
mindset, attracted it. The mind is a movement. The body is the manifestation
of movement. When we really get that, when, that sinks into that part of us
where we say we get it, then we could look at somebody else that is really
doing well, getting using their mind.

Never change things by fighting the existing reality...to change things, build a new model.

If you really wanna make a business rock, build a new model. Compensation comes fast if you start doing the right thing. Things start to change fast if you do the right things. You're gonna lay the foundation if you start fast. You see your LIFE changing right in front of your eyes.

We are programed to be broke; what we need to do is to find the frequency to vibrate like a BILLIONAIRE.

Everything is possible if you understand the universal law that determines how to vibrate like a BILLIONAIRE.

A BILLIONAIRE paradigm is a frequency to become a BILLIONAIRE. When I learned to control my paradigm / my habitual beheaviour, it helped me to do things, I did not want to do. I got in trouble because I knew how to do better financially, but my subconscious mind rejected the change. That used to be the problem that kept me stuck.

Paradigm is a hugh problem for everyone. Your paradigm has almost exclusive control over your broke beheaviour. You beheaviour that keeps you broke comes from your sub-conscious mindset. The enviroment you are living, is is the inspiration of your paradigm / habitual broke beheaviour.

Look at the ares of your LIFE that your paradigm / habitual beheaviour has enormous influence over.

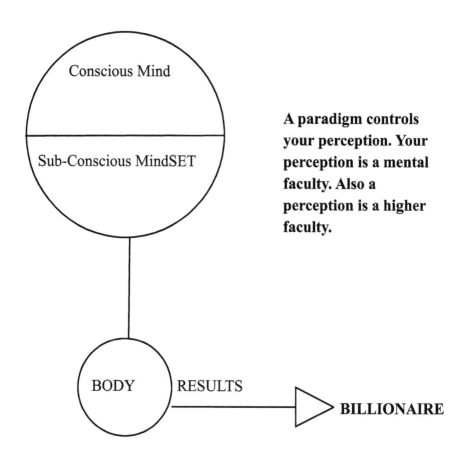

Conscious Mind

Sub-Conscious MindSET

A paradigm controls your perception. Your perception is a mental faculty. Also a perception is a higher faculty.

BODY RESULTS

BILLIONAIRE

Everything we don´t understand we have a tendency to critizise and redicure. Your paradigm controls when you become a BILLIONAIRE.

Your BILLIONAIRE paradigm controls your:

Perception

Use of time

Creativity

Effectiveness

Productivity

LOGIC

All the money in the world is available to us. All we need to do is earn it. And working a job seems to be the worst way to earn BILLIONS.

Billions of dollars hitting you in high quantities are never the RESULTS of hard work. BILLIONS come from the RESULTS of hard change of your paradigm / habitual behavior; it is the response of your subconscious mindset of definite demand based upon the application of definite principles, and not by chances or luck.

If you do what you are supposed to do, if you wanna change your subconscious mindset to become a BILLIONAIRE, your friends, relatives, may think you are crazy. You can't afford to listen to them. They try to talk you out of your dream to RESULT as a BILLIONAIRE.

If you change your perception, your income, your subconscious mind changes forever.

The truth is, you truely can create your own economie wealth LIFE, you can even have your own Boeing-747 aeroplane. You don´t have to depend on what your friends, parents are saying. To be able to shape your future, you have to be willing and able to change your paradigm / habitual behavior. Your habitual behavior should be the vibration of a BILLIONAIRE.

If you don´t change your habitual behavior, you never gonna get a new billion dollar RESULT.

Leaders are readers and learners

It is the positive repetition that puts you into an active leading position. If you repeat reading this book at least one-hundred times, you can't help that this book drops into your subconscious mindset.

Learning means you constantly entertain an idea, you get emotionally involved in that idea, you act on the idea and you change the end RESULT, get the feedback from the change = RESULTS.

You must learn and repeat to learn how to become a BILLIONAIRE, if you wish to have the RESULTS of a BILLIONAIRE.

The conscious mind means you have the ability to choose. If you choose what steps into your sub-Conscious mind, you automatically choose what drops into your subconscious mind, that controls your habitual beheaviour.

If you constantly choose to spend time reading books written by a BILLIOANIRE and you choose to stay away from trash TV, your body reacts and starts to vibrate on the sub-consciousness and frequency of a BILLIONAIRE. The RESULT can't be any other than being a BILLIONAIRE. We have the ability to reject or accept whatever we hear, see, touch or smell. If you don't wanna touch an ugly looking woman you wouldn't consider to do it. Reject what you don't like and embrace what makes you vibrate. Your sub-conscious mind / paradigm must accept; if you only give it the concept and the learning structure of a BILLIONAIRE.

The paradigm / your habitual behavior controls the RESULTS.

You are not a BILLIONAIRE because your financially broken paradigm / habitual behavior is the problem. It is the conditioning of your sub-conscious mindset.

How you set your sub-conscious mind dictates your ability to RESULT as a BILLIONAIRE.

All you need is a winnig attitude if you wish to earn billions.

If you wish to earn billions before you turn twenty years of age you must have a winning attitude. If you have the ability to win your paradigm / habitual beheaviour is going to find a way to RESULT as a BILLIONAIRE. With a proper consistent, constant change you gonna RESULT as a BILLIONAIRE.

Using drugs is a system, and behind it is a cause.

We don´t have an alcohol problem, we don´t have a cause, we don´t have a drug problem, we don´t have a relationship problem, we don´t have a productivity problem, the only problem we ever have is SELF - image / SELF - respect problem. Our SELF image / SELF - respect problem sets the boundariesof our performances in our LIFE. We can´t out-perform our SELF image. Our image is the govenor that sets the boundaries of performance in each and every area of our LIFE.

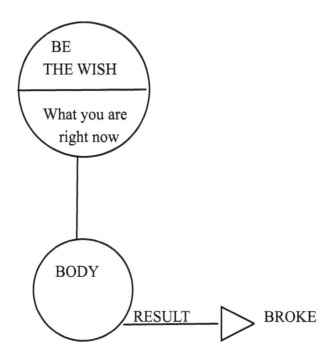

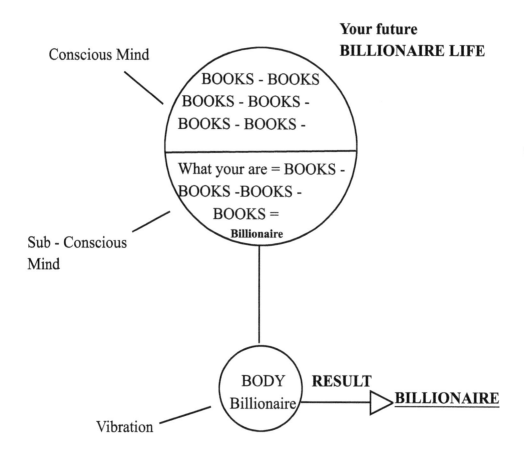

Things seemed never really to happen in my LIFE.

Why?

Then I could see clearly what was wrong with me and it would only take me three years to straighten my subconscious mindset. I started to see doors instead of silent walls.

- **YOU** can change your income by the way **YOU** change your income.
The law of repetition fixes to change the RESULTS of your income. Constant, consistent, repetition is the number of times. Through constant, consistent repetition you develop the habitual behavior. If you practice constant repetition long enough, your habitual behavior RESULTS in billions.
What are you willing to give or to give up to have what you WANT?
Nature's greatest law is the law of cause and effect. The great universal law says: "You can´t take more out of LIFE than you put into it. Why is it then that we don´t achieve the universal billion dollar goal?
It is because of the universal reason that it is called FEAR.
Fear = failure is the reason most people don't try to do things. What if I try and fail?

Example: You go to a dance club and you visualize a wonderful woman. You wanna approach her and ask for a dance. But you are afraid to walk across and ask for the dance.You are afraid (FEAR) of her reaction.

RESULTS in control of **"YOU"** vs. **"YOU"** in control of RESULTS = Being a BILLIONAIRE.

We must have a purpose in our LIFE. We must have a burning flame in our soul that warms us.

The question is: "Why are you here on planet earth?

You were fashioned by The Lord to have a rich LIFE full of abundance.

Things seemed never really to happen in my LIFE.

Let me tell you how you overcome the FEAR of failure: "You need to set a goal that is worth failing for.

Why is it that most people don't pursue their dreams? Because they didn't know how to do it. The reason we don't pursue possibilities is because subconsciously we don´t believe that it can happen for us; we don´t believe that we deserve it. How much time do you spend working on you? How much time do you spend working on your dream to become a BILLIONAIRE? In the last ninety days, how many books have you been reading? During the last year, what new skills or knowledge have you acquired? What kind of investment have you made to re-shape your subconscious mindset. I you want to make it today you must run towards your destiny if you wish to become a BILLIONAIRE, you must make some conscious effort to develop your subconscious mindset if you wish to vibrate like a BILLIONAIRE.

Fear, limited vision and a lack of SELF - Esteem is what keeps most people doing things they don´t wanna do.
A new BILLIONAIRE LIFE comes from a new subconscious mindset. You can´t step into your new BILLIONAIRE future, but remain in your broken financial pattern. You must kill the old - YOU - immediately.
Are you committetd to change your subconscious mindset like an athlete who plays like LeBron James, without being committed, nothing happens, nothing changes in your LIFE. You are not committed to the frequency to become a BILLIONAIRE; you are not gonna become the vibration of a BILLIONAIRE; and you are not gonna RESULT as a BILLIONAIRE.
You have to be committed through the storm, through the pain, through the rain, through the pain, and through the pain of disappointment. The journey of a BILLIONAIRE is a commitment and not a feeling. Until you have the taste of finishing, you will not vibrate in the frequency of respecting yourself as a BILLIONAIRE. You must win the battle against your own broken subconscious mindset.

Do you have the courage to act consciously on what you see in your fantasy?

It takes courage to become a BILLIONARE. If you don't wanna set a new frequency to vibrate like a BILLIONAIRE, because the vibration produces a new wave, I say: "Stay mediocre, be normal, be boring, just fit in. And if you are concerned about people that nutrlize your dream to become a BILLIONAIRE - just fit in with everybody else. Dress like everybody else, walk like everybody else, act like everybody else, eat like everybody else, go where they go, think ike they think, do what they do...-and once you neutralize your uniqueness to become a BILLIONAIRE...-you see you don't need courage.

It takes courage to have a big dream, it takes courage to be different, it takes courage to go where you have never gone before, it takes courage to be a billion dollar success, it takes courage to win. People don't talk about someone who does not win. If you win, they talk about you. It takes courage to step on the frequency to be exceptional; it takes courage to think big.

In this weak, watered down, mediocre society that we live in today, in this trash REALITY-TV-WORLD we are living in these days - I'm wondering if there is anybody left that's got the courage to say after all I have been through, and all my ancestors have been through, and all my parents have been through, - I did not come through all of that just to fit in with mediocre. - I HAVE THEN COURAGE TO BECOME A BILLIONAIRE.

Do you have the courage to act consciously on what you see in your fantasy? It takes courage to become a BILLIONARE. If you don't wanna set a new frequency to vibrate like a BILLIONAIRE, because the vibration produces a new wave, I say: "Stay mediocre, be normal, be boring, just fit in. And if you are concerned about people that nutrlize your dream to become a BILLIONAIRE - just fit in with everybody else. Dress like everybody else, walk like everybody else, act like everybody else, eat like everybody else, go where they go, think ike they think, do what they do...-and once you neutralize your uniqueness to become a BILLIONAIRE...-you see you don´t need courage.

It takes courage to have a big dream, it takes courage to be different, it takes courage to go where you have never gone before, it takes courage to be a billion dollar success, it takes courage to win. People don´t talk about someone who does not win. If you win, they talk about you. It takes courage to step on the frequency to be exceptional; it takes courage to think big. In this weak, watered down, mediocre society that we live in today, in this trash REALITY-TV-WORLD we are living in these days - I'm wondering if there is anybody left that´s got the courage to say: "After all I have been through, and all my ancestors have been through, and all my parents have been through, - I did not come through all of that just to fit in with mediocre. - I HAVE THEN COURAGE TO BECOME A BILLIONAIRE."

Without goals you go no places, without goals you can't achieve whatever you want. It's very important to think of what you want. This is what we really wanna get straight.

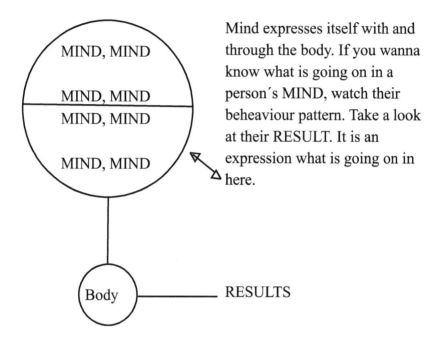

Mind expresses itself with and through the body. If you wanna know what is going on in a person's MIND, watch their beheaviour pattern. Take a look at their RESULT. It is an expression what is going on in here.

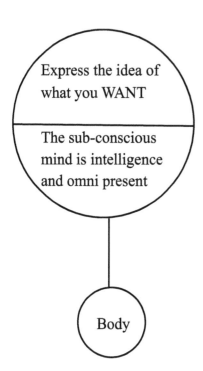

Express the idea of what you WANT

The sub-conscious mind is intelligence and omni present

Body

Example: Let´s suppose I give you a call while you are in Baghdad and I am in New York. I can get you on the other end of the telephone line / frequency, it looks like we are a long way apart, but that is an illusion. The case is we are on the same frequency; that's why we can have a chat over the telephone.

Understand that everything is frequency; it is a universal law, knowledge, intelligence. Every power is about knowledge; money is about knowledge.
If you impress that idea upon your subconscious mind, you attract everything that is in harmony with it. If you can phone with some in Bagdad while you are in New York, it means the frequency is in harmony, it can attract the other telephone.

If you are not responsible for your choices who should be respnsible for his choices

When you express that idea and you stay emotionally involved with that idea, that idea changes everything in your phsical world. Your physical vibration changes, you change what you attract into your LIFE. You change your behavior; ultimately you change your RESULTS = BIILIONAIRE.

Wake up your subconscious BILLIONAIRE mind and you are going to get it. Decide what you WANT / LOVE doing and commit to do it for REST of your LIFE = RESULT.
The problem with most people is they don't know what they LOVE doing. They THINK of it.
I know what I WANT to do; I WANT to RESULT for the REST of my LIFE on the frequency of a BILLIONAIRE. It's got to be my habitual behavior. I cut everything off that does not serve my purpose to RESULT as a BILLIONAIRE.

Being a BILLIONAIRE is a 1% strategy and 99% mindSET = how you set your subconscious mind / habitual behavior to achieve your goal to RESULT as a BILLIONAIRE. Your sub-conscious mind is screwing you, if you think you can't achieve your dream to RESULT as a BILLIONAIRE. Don't waste your time on strategies, it is all about to set the sub-conscious mind straight. Most people don't take charge of their success, they don't even know who the director of their LIFE even is. I suggest you become the master of your LIFE. Who should be in charge of your financial future if not your mind / sub-subconscious mind / habitual beheaviour. You decide exactly what you WANT & I show you with this book series how to vibrate as a BILLIONAIRE.

DECIDE WHAT KIND OF LIFE YOU WANT AND SAY NO TO EVERYTHING THAT ISN'T THAT.

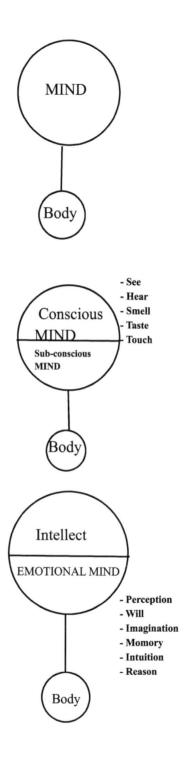

The emotional mind is where your habitual behavior is your paradigm. You have hooked up in your intellectual mind, higher faculties and these are what separates you from all the rest of the animal Kingdom. The animal kingdom operates by instincts which are perfect.

You have to use these as tools to RESULT as a BILLIONAIRE:

Perception

Will

Imagination

Momory

Intuition

Reason

These tools have the ability to change your paradigm forever.

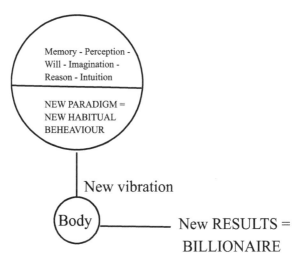

Memory - Perception - Will - Imagination - Reason - Intuition

NEW PARADIGM = NEW HABITUAL BEHEAVIOUR

New vibration

Body ———— New RESULTS = BILLIONAIRE

The vibration dictates what comes into your LIFE.
Power is the vibration of energy. A book is power and knowledge.

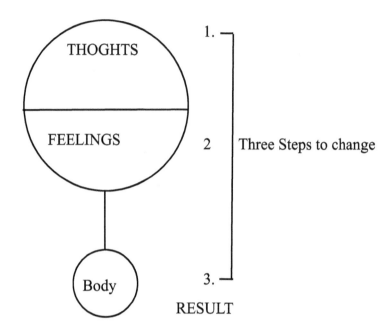

The attitude is the composite of your thoughts, your feelings and your actions; you choose your thoughts or you gonna accept the thoughts of somebody else. Your thoughts causes your feelings, those feelings expressed through your body determines the RESULT.

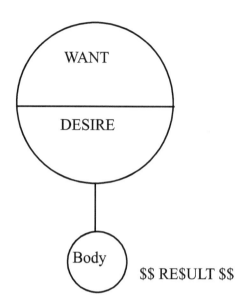

Let's talk about what we want. The WANT will turn into a desire.
Desire is the effort of the unexpressed possibility of the WANT, within the
expression of the united unexpressed possibility, within seeking expression,
without through your action. See, if you want to build a desire, you build the
desire by holding onto the picture of what you want and letting yourself get
emotionally involved in it.

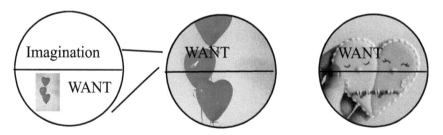

The heart is the devine side of your persoanlity. This is where the WANT
originates.

It´s the spirit it´s the dynamique power within you, that is going to cause you to activate your imagination. The WANT comes from inside = the heart and from the spiritual essence of who you are, and it steps into the consciousness; it activates your imagination and the WANT grows in your consciousness.

Take the WANT and turn it back over to the heart - to the infinite power within you.

As you express the idea, the WANT turns into DESIRE, the DESIRE alters the vibration you are in, the vibration causes the action, the action causes reaction, that reaction causes a change, that change causes the conditions, the circumstances and the enviroment to change or if we put them all together you can say in the vernacular it changes the RESULTS. This is not a game we are playing this is serious business, this is your LIFE you are dealing with.

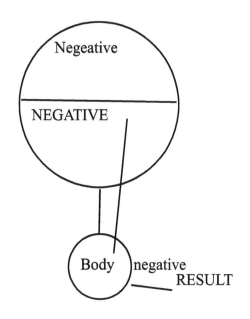

outside negative
world

Whatever is going on
in the outside world,
is coming into your
sub-conscious mind
and then it drops into
your sub-conscious
mind.

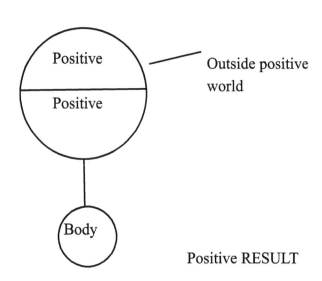

A-B-C of goals

C = Fantasy
B = What I think I can do
A = Present RESULTS

Goals are not there to get things; things are a side benefit; goals are here t grow. You have to go after bigger things, where you say: "I don´t know how to do it."
If your goal is an "A"-type goal something you have done in the past, won´t qualify as a goal.

Type - "B" is a -iF- goal: "If I have a side job and extra income, I can do XYZ. If my mother / father gives me extra money I can do XYZ.

Type - "C" = Fantasy = What you WANT = BILLIONAIRE. The case is you are taught not to fantasize like a kid. So you go back to "A" = Present RESULTS.

Type - "A" = is not a motivation.

If you wanna stick with "C" you must use your fantasy to get it.
The Wright brothers, those guys who invented the first aeroplane, had a fantasy. These brothers used all their imaginations to make the first plane fly. It took them, it took them twelve years. That's the fantasy that one day you are going to fly over the Atlantic Ocean to another country.

If you are going after what you really want you not gonna quitt.

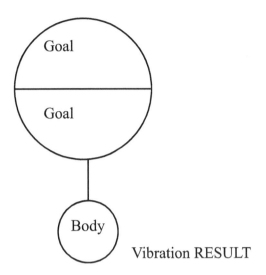

Goal

Goal

Body

Vibration RESULT

Know where you are going and know that you WANT get there the WANT to do it = Attitude.

Attitude is your WANT

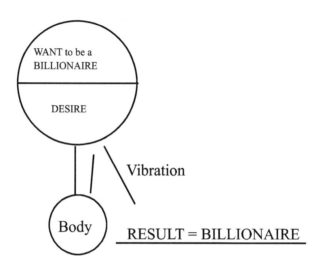

See, if a person really locks into what, they WANT, they vibrate and get emotionally involved in it. Everything is possible if you vibrate on your fantasy.

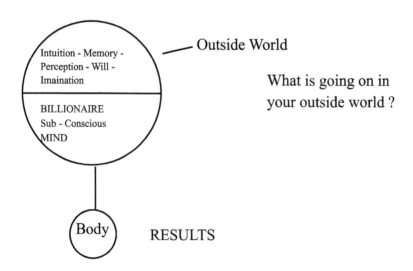

All things are possible if you decide what you WANT.

You WANT to buy a villa ?

Now, you're gonna say you don't have the money. You don't need the money. What do I mean? I said I made the WANT to buy a villa and start the vibration. Work with the power that is infinite. You are expressing that power yourself. What you don't know can kill you. You must start knowing. Don´t waste your time with: "I don´t know how?"

Be a goal achiever, that is your responsibility. You have to be disciplined, you have to have a great attitude, but all those things are not possible, if you don't have a definite goal you can chase after. If you have that definite goal you wake up in the morning, you are inspirered to attack the day because you wish to create something magic, becuase you have a goal / WANT to achieve.

If you are stuck you are operating with the wrong attitude or you don´t have a goal.

Say no to everything that does not bring you into the LIFE you wanna live. Be the person you WANT to become, if you WANT to vibrate and RESULT as a BILLIONAIRE. You can´t have your current broke attitude today, if you wanna grow as a BILLIONAIRE, become that paradigm / habitual behaviour that is going to RESULT as a BILLIOANIRE. Get your WANT and turn it into the frequency to DESIRE, the DESIRE to change your vibration is going to to RESULT = BILLIONAIRE.

You attract what you are in harmony with.

People accept the idea what they don´t WANT and internalize it, but we WANT to do the opposite. If you fall in LOVE with the frequency of your WANT the DESIRE to vibrate as a BILLIONAIRE , you can´t help but to vibrate as a BILLIONAIRE.

You are only limited by your weakness for attention. If you are overweight you are limited by the weakness of attention to care about the shape of your body, that's why your body is in bad shape. Just start to pay attention to what you eat. A lot of people think losing weight is going to happen automatically, use your attention and focus to lose weight. The same attention is needed if you wish to earn billions of dollars. If you are poor, you walk in the wrong direction. Your unapologetial attention creates everything for you. You don't have to sit on your hands and hope that one day you might lose weight or one day you might eran billions of dollars. Hope brings you no places other than being overweight or broke. Action is the only solution to your problem. Action takes you wherever you wish to go. Guess what, your attention gives you everything you WANT.

The law of vibration is the law of attraction if you have the attention to focus on your goals like a laser pointer.

The basket ball players Michael Jordan, Kobe Bryant, LeBron James, all of them, had something in common; all of them worked hard on their skills. The audience knew them for their work ethic. Kobe Bryant stood up at 04:00am to practice on his skills. Ask yourself the question: Do people know you for your work ethic? Talent won´t work if you WANT to win, work ethic is the action to win the game. Micahel Jordan showed up two hours earlier to make sure he could win the game, and also to make sure he was in physical condition to win the final.

The market is going to reward what you do every day. If you do nothing, the RESULT is going to be = ZERO.

You gonna die by yourself; you have to make billions by yourself, and you must confront the fears by yourself. You have to fight for your dream to RESULT as a BILLIONAIRE for yourself.

You must do more activities, you can't slow down. If you do slow down, the environment becomes a threat.

With whom you live with, sleep with, talk with, is going to affect your subconscious mindset. So pick someone and go deep.

The real you - who you are today, is a RESULT of a broken subconscious mindset. You have to become a new YOU, by exchanging your subconscious mind.

Get out of MAYBE-LAND and stay out of that MAYBE scenario forever.

You don´t need more ideas to become a BILLIONAIRE, just change your subconscious mindset.

Find something you are great at.

Don´t do business that does not serve your life. You are here to make money for a fantastic LIFE. Make hard decision fast. LIFE is short and tough. When things get tough, successful people make hard decision.

Total freedom comes from not having depts. You have to get addicted to something. I am addicted to my wife and my kids. What are you addicted to? Yes, of course I am addicted to my money.

We have more information available than ever in the history of the world.

If you really want your LIFE to be successful you can´t let your LIFE do certain things. Once you understand that you have a chance to find the path to your billion dollar success.

Being a successful BILLIONAIRE is a principle. The universal law of a BILLIONAIRE teaches us two exact rules. Rule number one don´t waste money rule number two follow rule number one. That is a universal principle to make it financially big. That rule is very simple but gets broken all the time.

The unknown seductive world is dangerous because it does not teach you how to be an independent thinker. You need to think for yourself; what it means to be a BILLIONAIRE.

The principle to become a BILLIONAIRE is a smart way to handle things over and over again in an excellente way.

There are principles for everything, how to win a formula one race, how to be the best rugby player, how to be the best piano player, how to be The King Of Pop.

You acquire knowledge from making mistakes, that´s where the lessons are hidden. If you lose your house, you need to reflect on why you lost your house. If you lose your income due to alcohol abuse, you need to do a reflection on it.

Truth is the essential foundation for producing good outcomes.

DREAMS + REALITY + DETERMINATION = A SUCCESSFUL LIFE

Those wo got it, Don´t need to prove they got it.

Unless you mastered sales you don´t have a business you have a hobby.

If you really want your LIFE to be successful, you can´t let your LIFE do certain things. Once you understand that, you have a chance to find the path to your billion dollar success.

I need to learn to escape the environment and the low subconscious mindset that surrounded me. I understand that till this day I have to think independently of myself. Some want a LIFE that is directed by others.

I decided till this day what works best for me. The courage to do it was also very challenging because the enviorment wantd to talk me out of my dream and make me confirm with their reality. Looking back on my journey to reach my dream of becoming a BILLIONAIRE, I see as time passes, LIFE is like a river. The river of live carries us with encounters with reality. Decision are needed while we go down our..

We can't avoid the encounters that happen in LIFE; we can only approach them in the best possible way. In your lifetime you will face millions of decisions. The quality of your good financial decisions will determine the quality of your LIFE. The most valuable things I have learned in my LIFE time were the RESULTS of my mistakes I reflected on. I formed principles from my learned mistakes. So I wouldn´t make the same mistake again and again. These principles took me from being a very ordinary man to becoming a BILLIONAIRE.

PAIN + REFLECTION = PROGRESS

My BILLIONAIRE SUCCESS is a RESULT of a unique approach to LIFE. I remember I started to embrace reality and confirmed to deal with it.

The billion dollar path you take in LIFE is your most important decision. I wanted my LIFE to RESULT as a BILLIONAIRE. I feared boredom and mediocrity more than I feared failure. Since I did not start out with money, all I needed was a bed to sleep in and a rest room. I went out to pursue my adventure to RESULT as a BILLIONAIRE. I went after the things I wanted and of course I failed; I had the discipline to get up again and crash again with my ideas. Each time I failed I learned my lessons. Then learned how to read books written by BILLIONAIRES; I studied those books; I crashed less. By doing that over and over again, I learned failure is where the lessons are hidden.

I learned that we have been given the law of the universe by mother nature. Humans did not create them, but we can use them to learn and grow. Realizing that you can trick mother nature and the laws of the universe made me a hyper-realist. It means I relized it´s better to work with other nature than against the most pwerful force on the planet. I stop making the laws of the universe "as I wish it should be". Working with the law is the truth of every BILLIONAIRE. Hyper realis is the best way to work with the laws of the universe that transform you into a BILLIONAIE.

Having big dreams plus embracing reality plus having a lot of determination automatically results into a successful LIFE = BILLIONAIRE. This formula is true for everyone.

To succeed we must embrace complete reality. Especially the harsh reality we wish weren´t true.

Problems - Mistakes - Weaknesses

Each of us has the unique capability to think logically, to reflect on ourselves and our circumstances, and to direct our own personal evolution.
Doing it well is just a matter of the five-step process.
We have already discussed how important it is to reflect carefully after experiencing pain.

Step 1: Know your goals and run after them. What is best for you depends on your nature, so you really need to understand who you are. Know what you want to achieve in LIFE.

Step 2: Encounter the problem that stands in your way of getting to your goals. These problems are typically painful. But to emerge into somthing higher you need to identify those problems and not tolerate them.

Step 3: Diagnose those problems. Find out where the root cause is hidden. Don't jump too quickly to solutions. Take a few steps back and reflect to really distinguish the symptoms from the disease.

Step 4: Design a plan to eliminate the problems. This is where you determine what you need to get around problems.

Step 5: Do it. Push yourself to progress toward your goal to RESULT as a BILLIONAIRE.

Bad things happen to all of us in LIFE. It can ruin us or build us stronger. Depending on how we handle them.

The most important principle I have already told you is to change your paradigm / habitual behavior; secondly, don´t waste money and thirdly is yet to follow: Management.

What should you study to become a BILLIONAIRE? My answer is to study business management and psychology.

Being a BILLIONAIRE is an administrator of money. The highest level to achieve financially is to become a BILLIONAIRE. A BILLIONAIRE is a manager of valuable resources. The key to maintaining your BILLIONAIRE status is the effective, consistent management, delegation, and distribution of resources. Broke people think that BILLIONAIRES operate in emotions; somehow they believe it.

They think a BILLIONAIRE can get anything he wants. That's why broke people are broke.

What causes crisis? Greed. Greed is the mis-management of resources of resources for personal benefit, that´s greed. A greedy spirit will manipulate resources so that he or she can be the ultimate benefit only. Greed is a Kingdom killer. A greedy person is an arrogant person.

Bernie Madoff was simply full of greed. He lost everything he thought was his LIFE. Now his LIFE is LIFE in prison.

A real Billionaire is financially smart.

The universal law stops anything from growing where there is no manager. If you don't take care of your plant in your apartment, it stops growing and it dies, if you don´t nurture your subconscious mindset to RESULT as a BILLIONAIRE, it will die with a broke financial mindset because you mismanaged the money.

You are overweight? The only individual who is to blame is the man in the reflection of the mirror. You are not a BILLIONIARE the only person to put guilt on is the man in the mirror. The only person that is standing in your way is YOU. Take control of your LIFE and stop blaming others for your recent RESULTS. If you don't know the law of how to RESULT and vibrate as a BILLIONAIRE, go out buy a book, and study the universal law that transforms you into a BILLIONAIRE. Xes, it takes discipline and a little bit of time. You can't achieve that goal within three weeks. The only possibility to make it as a BILLIONAIRE is to study and consistent repetition of the universal frequency of a BILLIONAIRE. Stop chasing the narrative that you can´t make it big in LIFE, because your environment teaches nothing of value. Remember, people can fly to the moon, because they have a WANT. Find your WANT. You have to develop the WANT to do it.

Nobody is going to support you on your journey only like-minded people. If you have the WANT to do it, the next step is to create the ability to create whatever you want in LIFE. You are not on planet earth to lead a mediocre, boring LIFE. You are supposed to be a rich, healthy, positive individual full of wisdom and knowledge. The only way to gain wisdom is through books and positive vibrations.
I feel so sorry for you guys if you think money comes in without changing the old subconscious mindset. Let me tell you something. It is impossible to gain money and to hold the money forever with a broken old paradigm / habitual behavior.

Before you try to make big money in this world, the very first step is to change your daily home from an untidy apartment into a positive vibration. Step on the frequency to clean and tidy up your home the best you can. Step on the frequency to clean your windows, the bathroom, the entrance hall, make your bed every morning, clean your shoes, clean the kitchen area ...etc...

You can´t win the billion dollar RESULT if you are always surrounded by a negative untidy home. That is simply impossible. You can´t match the frequency of a BILLIONAIRE if the vibration of your apartment is dirty. Instant actions is required and not slow preparations in the sense of: I'm going to do it tomorrow or next weekend.

You are supposed to live in a clean, beautiful home that sends positive vibrations. How can you send positive vibrations to attract customers if you live in a dirty apartment? It is just impossible.

Be the change, be the inspiration, the frequency, be the vibrations, be the clean gentleman in a clean environment / apartment. Just be the positive frequency of vibrations that can only RESULT as a future BILLIONAIRE.

A BILLIONAIRE is someone who knows values and collects the money / value. What I mean by that is: Don´t waste your time with uninspirational situations that keep you full of negativity and financially broke. You are here on planet earth to experience success in any form / shape and fashion.

You have to master the frequency of a BILLIONAIRE like a piano player masters his musical craft. See, The King Of Pop mastered his musical craft so well, that he sold more than three-hundred-million copies of the album called THRILLER. He started his music career at the age of four years young, and twenty years later, he transformed himself into the best selling musical artist the world has ever seen.

Don´t believe that you are not special. You win with your subconscious mindset. The power of your paradigm / habitual behavior brings you on the frequency to RESULT as whatever you wish vibrate. The biggest fear in LIFE is losing. The case is you only lose if you give up.

See, he was born in Gary, Indiana as a poor child.

The easiest thing in the world is to be negative and sad or to blame other people for your RESULTS.

I know it's tough to keep the discipline. The easiest thing in the world is to sit there and compare yourself to other successful people. It is your ability to understand that you have the same 24 Hours in LIFE like these BILLIONAIRE who already made it. Reach down deep and start to compete, by changing your paradigm. Nobody can motivate you but the man in the mirror.

Do you understand what the King Of Pop went through in his LIFE as a child, as a teenager, as an adult? They used to call him a Nigger, they used to call his mother a Nigger, they used to call him a pedophile, they used to call him ugly, do you understand that giving up was not an option for him? He had the WANT to succeed. See, again: change your paradigm. Don't be scared to fail. If you fail, see it as a lesson to grow. Remember, Thomas Edison needed to fail over two-thousand times before he found the right equation for how to make a light bulb work.

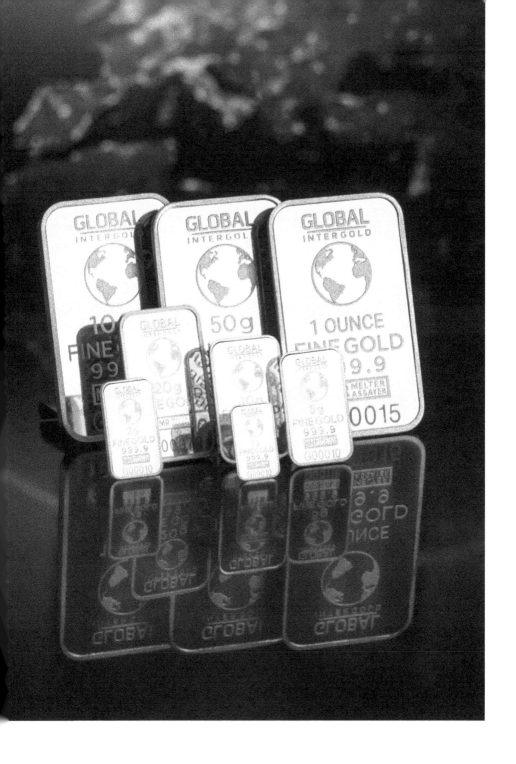

You have to work work hard to change your habitual beheaviour you must LOVE to change your paradigm. Work so much harder on your dream to RESULT as a BILLIONAIRE like LeBron James works to succed as the best basket ball player.

Learn to love to feed your mind with positivity.

Don´t be scared to try to change your paradigm. Trust me, it´s worth it. Stay away from the doom crowed provided by trash TV. Trust yourself that reality TV brings you no other than financial broke. Within thirty days from now, you're not gonna be the same person. You need stupid television programs like you need a damn whole in your brilliant mindset. You are here to vibrate like a BILLIONAIRE and not like these ignorant people in a trash TV show. Look for the good things by reading and studying the law of a BILLIONAIRE. You 've got to learn the complete opposite.

The doom and bloom crowded will tell you it won´t work. See, it does not work for them because they can't look into your mind.

You need to understand that your LIFE belongs to you. You are responsible for the good things and the bad things that happen. If you earn several billions, it was your responsibility. If you don´t that is your responsible RESULT.

Leading with your new paradigm / habitual behavior is the way to make it as a BILLIONAIRE. If you change your paradigm / habitual behavior, you gonna win as a BILIONAIRE. Changing the paradigm / habitual behavior is like to train a muscle.

If you want to build a great subconscious BILLIONAIRE mindset, you must dedicate your time to it like you train in a fitness studio. You have to develope the WANT to RESULT as a BILLIONAIRE.

All you need is a change for a change. But don´t believe the chanc comes around like a miracle. You have to be prepared when the opportunity is there, the catch, the change. By catching the change, you start to read books that give you the chance to understand opportunities.

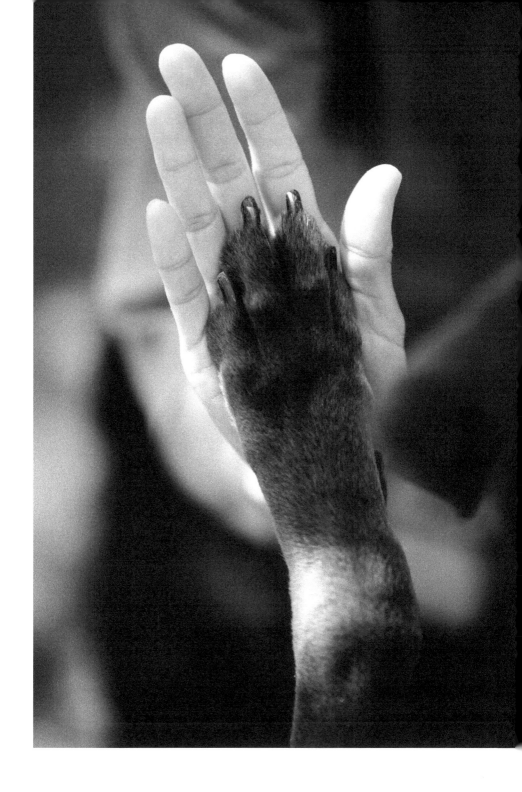

Your mind is srewing you. It WANTS to protect you from pain. It is very natural to feel uncomfortable every time a change is required. You are in a lie if your brain tells you you must wait until you feel alright for a change. The way our brain is wired , it is not designed to go through the unknown of a change. The problem is, you never gonna feel like it. Your brain teaches you it is easier to stay who you are.

We all have a habit of hesitation. Those few seconds of hesitating is the essence to protect you from pain and problems. If you change your desciosn to change your paradigm / habitual behaviour you change everything in your LIFE.
Be inspirered with a new habitual behaviour that lets you vibrate like a BILLIONAIRE.

At some point you have to start to change your habitual behaviour. Start to change your paradigm / habitual beheaviour by starting instantly with the uncomfortable things..

The gift of structure is the gift of every future BILLIONAIRE. If you wanna be the biggest BILLIONAIRE in the world, you got to study the frequency of the top ten patterns of the richest people, those who vibrate as BILLIONAIRES.

What are the similarities between those ultra-rich people? Saving money or wasting money? Go ahead and find out. What is the pattern of Warren Buffett? What is the Pattern of Bill Gates? What is the pattern of Elon Musk?

There is always the other side of the coin. Being a BILLIONAIRE comes with sacrificing your time to be a student of the greatest.

Whatever industry you pick to RESULT as a BILLIONAIRE, if you try to be better than the rest and try to out-work everybody, if you try to be a better salesperson than anybody, if you try to be better prepared than anybody, you got your best chance to RESULT as a BILLIONAIRE. Becuase if you don´t do it and somebody does, the chances are there that somebody tries to take that away from you. Learn to work with things as they are. Try to understand that someone working 24 hours takes things away from you.

The number one reason someone fails: Lack of effort and lack of brains. It means they don´t do the work and they are not willing to learn. Let me give you an example: When you start a business, you are never in a vacuum with no competition. There will always be competition; somebody will try to destroy your business. If you walk into a competitive environment they still know more about the business than you do, they know more about the customers, they are in better connection with the customers, they longer on the battle field of a business. You're gonna lose. Because you don't consider doing the work or learning more about the industry.

You have to put in the effort to learn more about your business - That´s the brains part and the effort part aswell. Because if you step into the environment of successful people, you are competing with the absolute very best. If you compete you better know what you are doing. Otherwise they gonna kick your butt out of business.

If you are not always learning till this minute and for the rest of your LIFE, how can you ever expect to RESULT as a successful BILLIONAIRE, somebody is going to kick you out of your dream of becoming a BILLIONAIRE. The greatest source of your future BILLIONAIRE LIFE should be knowledge. If you don´t have a thirst for learning and acquiring information, you are SOL

(Sadly - Outta - Luck).

What would you do to kick your butt to change your paradigm, and your habitual behavior forever? There is always someone who will criticize you or try to put you out of your business / dream, it´s better you figure out how they going to do it rather than they do it. You have to be paranoid and conscious of that competitive journey. You can´t downplay the competition. The world is what it is. Don't blame them for who they are. It´s just your fault if you don't do your homework. Be self-aware of what you are good at and what other people are good at. I mean, this is very helpful.

Learn how to learn. Learn how to learn to stick to your learnings. That is far more important to repeat consistently what should drop into your subconscious mindset.

Because the one certainty is that there will always be a change in business. If you don´t learn how to react to a change, you probably will fall out of business very soon. And if you don´t have a business that serves billions of people, you can´t vibrate and RESULT as a BILLIONAIRE.

Your BILLIONAIRE RESULT is a RESULT of learning how to aim for the frequency of a BILLIONAIRE. There is nothing you can´t accomplish in LIFE with the right amount of work.

Just go after your dream to vibrate as a BILLIONAIRE. Don´t make excuses. Why should you apologize if you WANT to RESULT as a BILLIONAIRE. The answer is it is your number one duty as a human being to work in order to have a rich LIFE full of abundance. You are not on planet earth to suffer from one pay check to the next pay check You are here to win YOUR dream and make YOUR dream a reality.
The reality has been already implemented in you. All YOU need to do is to birth that idea and make it a WANT.

History will always teach you great lesson who to do it and how to become the RESULT of a BILLIONIARE. You have got to find out what it takes to be a BILLIONAIRE by reading and consistent study the universal law of a BILLIONIARE. Enjoy the competiton ofexchanging your dump subconsciousmindset through a BILLIONAIRE mindset. The competition is going to be challengeing because you need the WANT to do it. Without the WANT, it´s a wish. A wish is for Santa Claus but not the reality of someone who WANTS to RESULT as a BILLIONAIRE.

Every time life gets harder you level up!

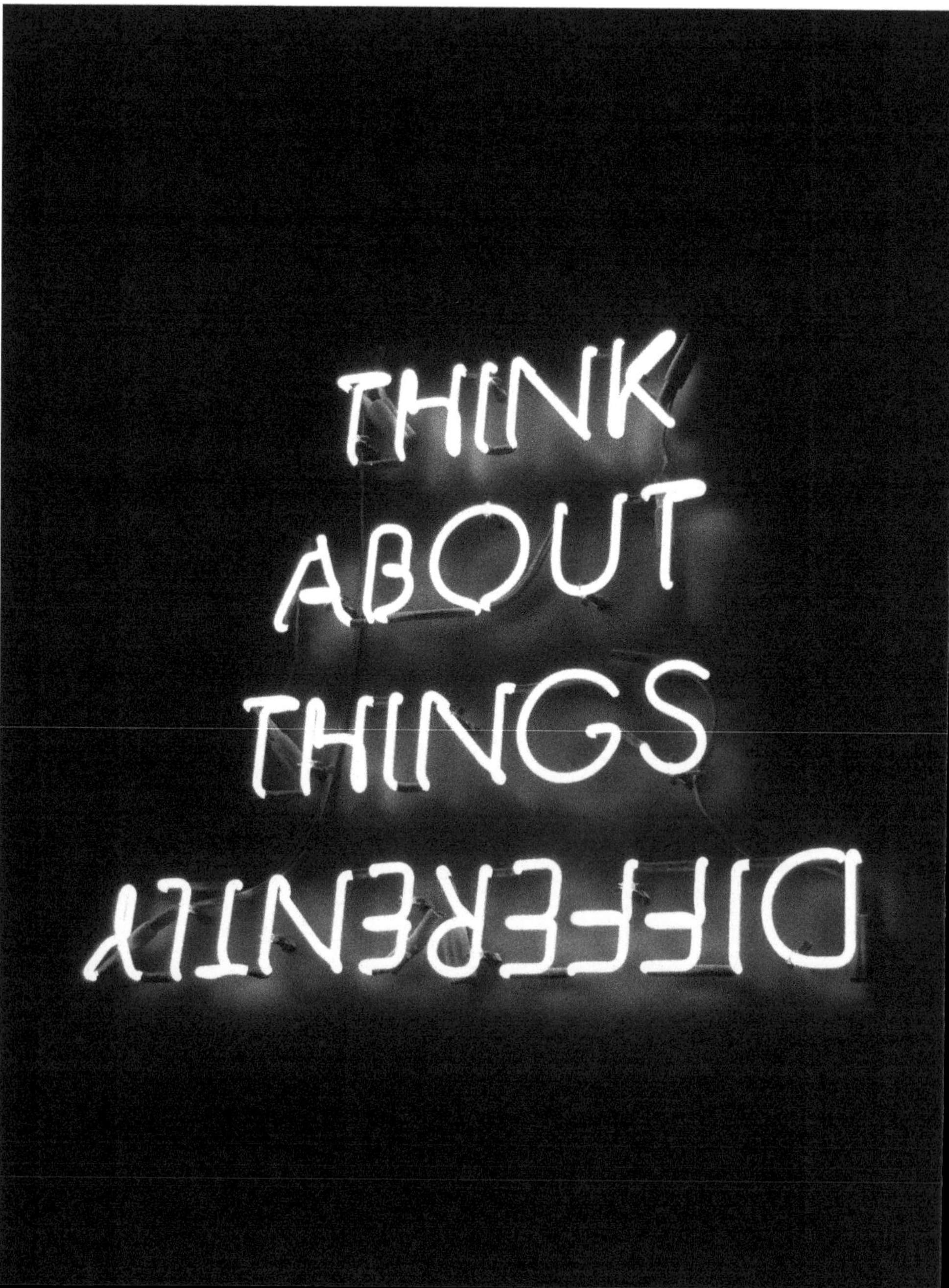
THINK
ABOUT
THINGS
DIFFERENTLY

Stop lying to yourself

You are here to change your broken subconscious mindset into a habitual RESULT of a BILLIONAIRE. Let me give you an example. If you have been a smoker for thirty years, you can't quit smoking within 24 hours. It takes at least three months or six months, or at least nine months to step away completely from cigarettes. The same with your new paradigm / habitual behaviour, it takes at leat 9nine month to re-program your mind into a thinking pattern of a BILLIONAIRE. Thus, stop lying to yourself and stop convincing the world that you already know the answer. Enjoy the procedure that changes your paradigm / habitual beheaviour.

You new subconscious mindset must be ready to compete with the absolute best on people on planet earth. Trust me they work and wake up very early to compete against you. It is nothing personal it ´s just strickt business to succes as the best on planet earth. If you look at your change as a job you already lost. It´s not gonna be your passion, you gonna count the time, you gonna count the pages you should read, you gonna count the pain you go through. You have to go all the time at least 360 days the extra mile if you wish to succed as a BILLIONAIRE. Without the extra mile you can vibrate and RESULT as a future BILLIONAIRE, that´s simple. Look at your change as something your enjoy to do. See the transformational process a beautiful journey that is going to let you vibrate as a BILLIONAIRE. The change will compliment you sooner or later if you put enough effort into it.

A BILLIONAIRE mindset means being the absolute best in the world. Whatever industry you are in. All you do as a BILLIONAIRE is consistent learning. It does not even matter if you fail thousands of times. Remember how much effort Thomas Edison needed. A winner outworks everyone even through his failure. A real winner keeps on going. You have to try different things, different income streams, even if 99% of them fail. You have to be right only one time. You can pick the wrong job (just over broke); you can pick the wrong spouse. You get your RESULT it right one time? You win. But if you don´t try all these different things, you never gonna get that "ONE TIME MOMENT".

Be curious about business, be curious about technology, be curious about LIFE, be curious about how the financial system works in total, try to understand the history of money. That curiosity gives you the advantage of being driven to RESULT as a BILLIONAIRE. Always learn and try to find new things. Start to build a network of like-minded people that supports you in your journey to become a BILLIONAIRE.

Try to understand why you wanna RESULT as a BILLIONAIRE. Put yourself in the shoes of a BILLIONAIRE and try to understand why they wanted to succeed as a BILLIONAIRE. If you do something that reflects society in the future, you're gonna succeed and automatically RESULT as a BILLIONAIRE. Bridge the gap between you and your followers. Make it easy for them to ask you questions. The more people you help, the more they are willing to recommend your service.

Thomas Edison got his job done because he had a vision. He never had his focus on the obstacles, in the sense that this was difficult. He saw opportunities to give the world light with the invention of the light bulb. Instead of coming up with: "I wish it would be easier. He said: "I wish I would be better." Even when his factory burned down he was so optimistic: "Thanks God, all my mistakes have been burned to the ground. " Rather finding an excuse he found always a way to make things work through failure. You have to accept the failure as a lesson to learn how an idea can´t work. If you fail it only teaches you that you need to give a try into another direction.

Your sourrounding will do a lot of talking but not any support that guides you into the right direction. Make a not to talk to list. That is crucially important because their actions and talking is going to affect your subconscious mindset. And if it does your dream to RESULT as a BILLIONAIRE in danger. Remember there is nothing you can´t accomplish in LIFE with the right amount of work. The challenge is still are you willing to have the WANT to do the work to RESULT as a BILLIONAIRE?

Being a BILLIONAIRE is all about prepartion. The process to fail is a preparation to do it better. Trust me it is hard to fail two-thousand times and still failing one-thoussand times again. If you don´t LOVE what you do to RESULT as a BILLIONAIRE your subconscious mindset will talk you out of your dream. Don´t follow the passion to bescome a BILLIONAIRE, follow the effort and the extra mile you need to go if you WANT to succed as a BILLIONAIRE. Your passion is a feeling. And feelings are there to protect your subconsciousness from the pain. Yoour feeling are there to comfort you and as we learned comfort is the enemy of every big BILLIONAIRE success. When you good at something you won´t quitt. Because nobody quits on something he enjoys doing.

Most people are concerned what the world might think about their dream to RESULT as a BILLIONAIRE. If these people are not on your frequency to vibrate as a BILLIONAIRE, why do you care about their opinion?

Just keep on grinding to pursue your billion dollar dream. Suddenly you appear as an overnight success. Keep on trying new things. Once you feel success, you feel it does not matter what your so-called friends think. It´s only important what your customers think, your business partners, all those who give you moeny to RESULT as a BILLIONAIRE. Why do you care what other people think. Do they pay for your meal? No, they don't pay for your meal? It means these ignorant people are not in charge of your life. They only line up to criticize your ideas? You know what you have to do.

Be on your focus like a laser pointer. The more focused you are, the higher the chance you point out your target to succeed. What do customers WANT from you as a business man except being honest. They WANT the feeling that you care about them 24/7. It does not matter if you sell one single product to each customer; what you need is the idea to make the customer WANT more. If they WANT more of your products, they spend more, if they spend more, you automatically make more money, if you make more money, your chances are there to RESULT as a BILLIONAIRE.

Your task is to put everybody and everything in the right position to RESULT as a BILLIONAIRE. And that success starts with new subconscious habitual behavior. You have to have a completely different structured daily LIFE of actions.

I am a book junkie; I enjoy walking through book stores. I read several hours every day. There is not a single day whitout reading a book. Meanwhile I don´t consider to say I read books, I prefer to say I study books by re-reading a book a least one-thousand times. See, what am I suppose to do with trash TV and gossip on TV. These so-called celebrity news brings you no place than being subconsciously stupid minded. Everything that is related to business read it and re-read it until it drops into your subconscious mindset. Try to find books written by BILLIONAIRES, about finance, about how to keep a business focus, how to save the moeny. You friends might thing you are crazy, because you still don´t follow my advise to create a "Not To Talk" list. If you read things that is in your interest you find it easier to step into your dream to achieve the bigger billion dollar dream. Once you find your unique finger print the only thing you ought to do is to repeat it on a consistent level. If you are good at repaeting it, the next step is can you be great at it?

Be a shark when it comes to learn, grap the opportunity to learn through reading. But understand that you don't learn by reading a book one single time, the essence of all books drops into your subconscious mind if you repeat it on a consistent basis.

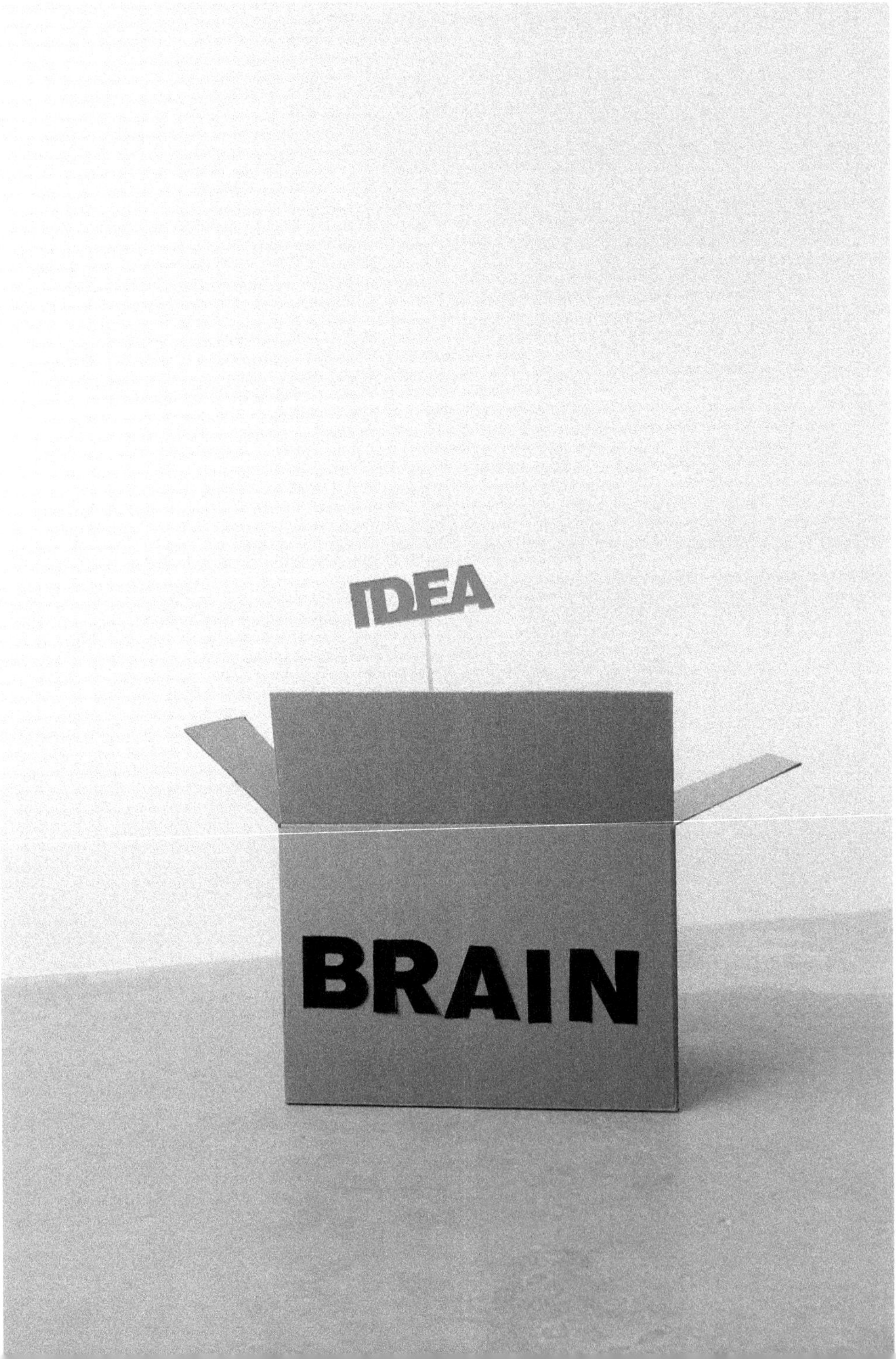
IDEA
BRAIN

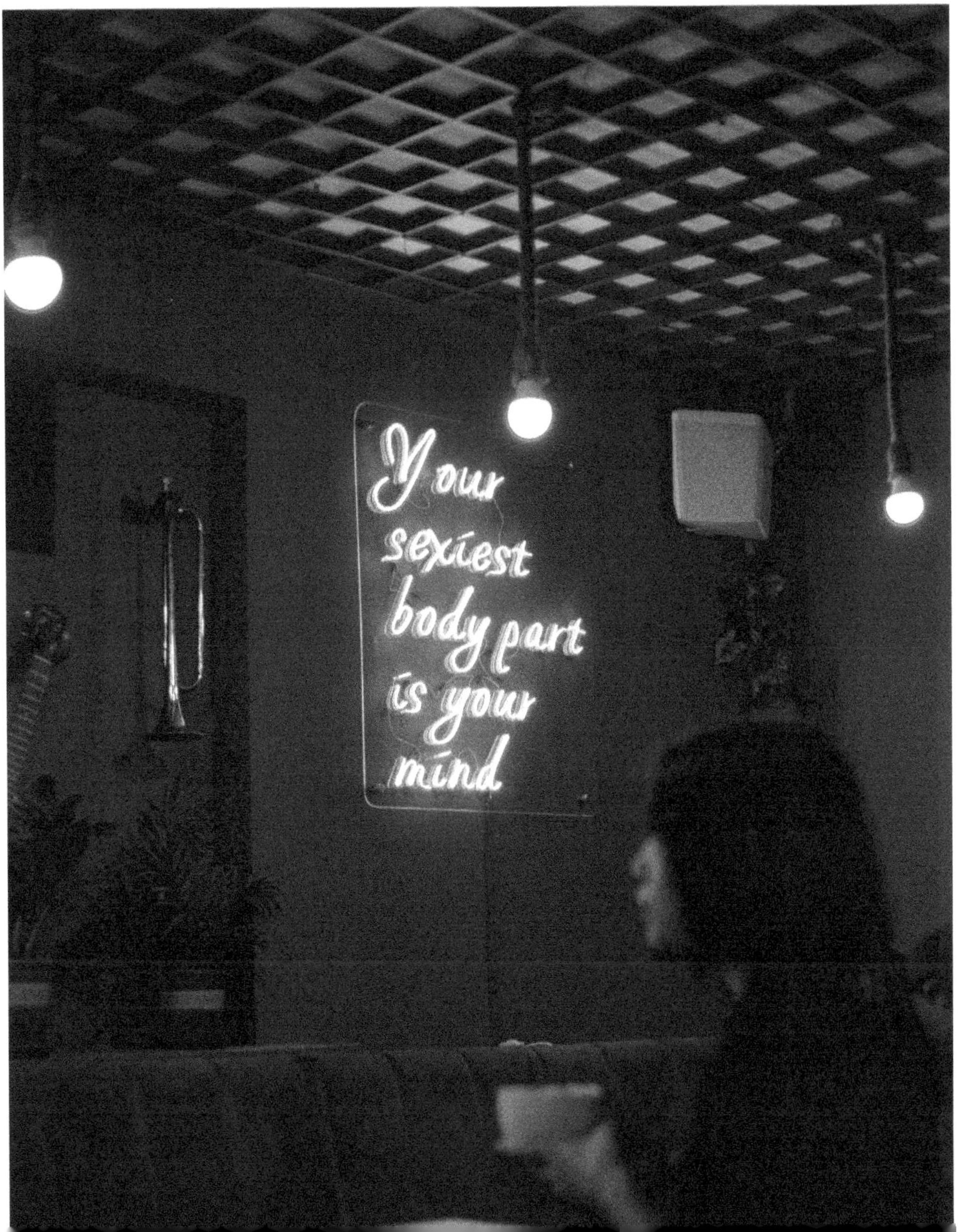
Your
sexiest
body part
is your
mind

If you really wish to RESULT as a BILLIONAIRE, pay off your debts. Because negativity holds you back from being in a positive financial environment. Be merciless regarding depts. There is no mercy to accept negative depts. A good loan is if you can pay it off within twenty four months. Everything else is bad for your financial situation. I know it's difficult. I have been there. I remember I returned home and there was no electricity; the police were after me becuase I owed the govement money. See, it´s not always easy.

Pay for everything by cutting the cost if you wish to step to the next level. What I did, for example, I reduced my electricity bills by switching the lights off every time I went into another room of my apartment. I went literally on the frequency to save money by not wasting the vibration of electricity. I stop using my car for everything that had to be done. I choose to ride as often as I could a bicycle. All that saved me money to pay off my negative depts.

You don´t need to look for a new income stream by appling for a new job, just be conscious about your daily wasting of money through your utility bills. Be supportive with your bank-account. Save money whenever you can. If you don´t know that a business is all about making and saving money you gonna fail until you understand that you have to take control over the outgoing money. The more you save, the more you benefit. Control your effort to be in control of your outgoing money. Without savings you can´t invest into your billion dollar DREAM to RESULT as a BILLIONAIRE. Thus, get off your ass and switch off the lights in the other room where you are not in right now! You don´t need to read a book in a room full of christmas ligtening. All you need is a single little lamp that provides enough light for your book readings. If you don´t understand the purpose of saving money, you won´t be able to make big billion dollar business.

Only poor people do linear work!

You have to have a better financial understanding of what saves you money and what brings you income and what steals your money away. Allow me to give you another example: Stop buying flowers for women. Why? See, these flowers are going to die very soon. You set them into a vase and after three weeks she has to throw them away. I tell you it´s better to buy her a watch or a book. Always be a student regarding saving coins. Be tactical enough to understand what is a waste and what is a saving / investment.

Being a BILLIONAIRE is a process. Once you understand that idea, you win subconsciously on every level of money. Create a positive environment that the money pops in automatically = The Law Of Attraction.

Sales cures it all. Have you ever heard of a business that had zero sales? If you don´t sale you don´t have a business. If you don´t sale, you don´t serve and attract billions of people. If you don´t attract billions of people, you never gonna have the chance to Result as a BILLIONAIRE.

Every business out there is in the buy low and sell high business.

RESULT as a BILLIONAIRE. You have to sell your idea, your product, your unique service. That is, the only key to having a billion dollar business is to do sales. Just do it yourself. Do not ask your friends for help.

What is selling? Selling is not to convince the customer, to sell means to help the customer. Either you make your customers LIFE easier or you make the LIFE of a customer boring. Follow the effort to inspire your customers. If they feel good about your product, they're gonna buy it the second time. And that is where you wanna be: In the after-sales business of being recommended. Your very good reputation brings you to a higher supreme BILLIONAIRE level. If you put your time in to supporting your customers as much as you can, you get better at it. If you get better at it, you become great in their eyes. And if you are great, you are considered a valuable brand to be trusted. That trusted brand is a recommendation that earns billions of money.

Care about your customer during the after-sales business. The after-sales process is crucially important. Stay in touch with your customers, send them a gift card during Christmas time. The efford means so much in these days of superficial social media where nobody does really something meaningful. It is going to be amazing how passionate your customers can get if you care about them during Christmas time or even when they have a birthday to celebrate. Your customers are in charge to see the greatness in your service, product.

You have to do things that nobody does in the after-sales business regarding caring about your customers. Give them the feeling that you will never leave them alone. Psychologically they gonna feel attracted to you =The law of attraction = The RESULT of a BILLIONAIRE.

Prepare to win more customers. The more customers the more money. Passion is the first step to becoming a BILLIONAIRE. But it is the effort to change your paradigm / habitual beheavior, to maintain your stauts as a BILLIONAIRE until you die. When you are dead, what are you gonna do with the money? Yes, that´s correct you can´t take it with you when you make your earthly transaction. How about to lay the foundation for a dynasty?

Your BILLIONAIRE status means nothing if you can pass it on to the next generation. See, how important it is to create value?
The most valuable thing next to your health and your new subconscious mindset is going to be your family structure. The idea of being a BILLIONAIRE is great, but are you willing to prepare the next generation to think and act like BILLIONAIRES?
Do you know what makes a dynasty great? If you don´t know the greatness of a dynasty study the Vanderbilts. That is the perfect blueprint for a dynasty. Yes, you need to read books written about the Vanderbilts, and re-read the book again and again. And yes, it is work. Don´t be afraid to work if you wish to change your paradigm.

Consistency is the key

Cornelius Vanderbilt came from humble beginnings; he was a tough business man, they say tough as steel nails. He laid the foundation for several generations after him. Do you know how many failures Cornelius Vanderbilt needed to face? Today it's not an option to highlight his failure. What you need to understand is the fact that he RESULTED as a SUCCESS.

If failure is not an option, you can´t improve from being medicare. Innovation goes through the procedure of failures. No mistakes no innovations. The big winners in this world paid for thousands of failed experiments.
If you do something in a new way, people are initially going to mis-understand you. Because they don't know better. If you never wanna be criticized stop being an independent thinker and innovator.

People go broke by trying to look rich.

You wanna change your paradigm into a billion dollar mindset?
From being broke to the RESULT of a BILLIONAIRE is a change of your paradigm / habitual behavior. Make it your habitual behavior to care about the money first by reducing the outgoing money.
You can only attract to you what you are in harmony with. If you wanna have health, you must be in harmony with it. If you want money, you must be in harmony with it. If you wanna RESULT as a BILLIONAIRE, you must be in harmony with it.

If you wanna attract billions, you must be in harmony with those who WANT to give you billions of dollars. Mutual attraction is the law of every successful BILLIONAIRE. Negative vibrations does not sell any product. The real reason Warren Buffett is the second richest man in the wolrd is he attracts the money into his LIFE by keeping it? How? He does not waste big money. Change your paradigm to attract the most money from your customers.

You can´t create billions without being full of discipline.
Discipline is important to your attitude; your thinking, it is important to your personal standards; discipline is important to how you start today; you have to understand how important discipline in general is.
Have the discipline to be the best regarding re-programing your subconscious mindset into a paradigm of a BILLIONAIRE.
Go really deep into the task to change your paradigm / habitual behavior. You discipline your mind to learn, it drops into your subconscious mind; your paradigm / habitual behavior controls your actions to earn billions of dollars. You can´t have great personal billion success if you are not disciplined to exchange the old paradigm with a new habitual behavior. Success is already in you. All you need to do is to trigger the frequency that you can vibrate like a big BILLIONARE.

Only invest in things you understand.

Competing with yourself is the ultimate positive sum - game!

Am I buying this with my time or are my assets paying for it.

A paradigm shift is a design of a resourceful enviorment where people from around the world collabrate, mastermind and explore opportunities independance by establishing multiple sources of income.

I remember I was earning over one billion dollars a year. Through a stream of over one-hundred income opportunities. I discipline myself to work and to study books by re-reading each books at least one-thousand times.

Being a BILLIONAIRE is a skill like typing. You can learn to have a BILLIONAIRE paradigm by consistent repetition.

Think and Grow Rich by Napoleon Hill means learn to think how to become rich. Thinking is not really taught in school. What is required in order to think effectively. Most people are lost when it comes to think, work and read effectively. You have to have multiple sources of

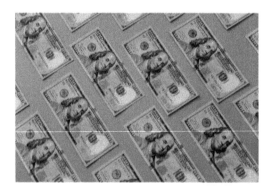

ncome.

Go always forward. Don't look to the side or left or right. Take a step into the future and not backwards. Let's go means to step out from the negative environment with zero RESULTS into a positive billion dollar business. Do the work to serve one billion people so that your bank account can vibrate on the level of a BILLIONAIRE. Lock yourself into your dream of a mindset of a BILLIONAIRE. That means turning off trash TV and studying the universal law of a BILLIONIARE. You have to go to the library and do some research on what it takes to be a BILLIONAIRE. You don't have time for trash TV. Because you need to catch your billion dollar success. The mindset is you can't be a dreamer anymore. You have to transform yourself into a realist.

You are already born where the odds are against you. You have to work harder than anybody by studying the law of a BILLIONAIRE; much harder than anybody else. The road to the best is to exchange your old RESULTS from being broke into the RESULT of a BILLIONAIRE. Go on your journey to find the positive energy that attracts BILLIONS. Educating yourself means studying, reading and re-reading and re-studying what you learned until you master the law of a BILLIONAIRE.

Don't work for your BOSS work for billions of people that are willing to pay for your idea.
Start investing into your subconscious mindset like a BILLIONAIRE. The dumpest thing you can do is waste your LIFE on a YOUTUBE loop or trash TV.

87% of humanity are unhappy. Why? Because they don't have what they perceive as what they deserve, but it's not what you deserve in LIFE; it's what you earn in LIFE.
I was born into an abusive household full of violence. My mother used to beat me; my father used to beat me every day with a belt. During my teenage years I went through a lot of trouble; incl., that I went three times into a foster home. While I was in a foster home I found out at the age of 17 years young, that if I WANT a better car, a better house,

I have to have good grades. If I have good grades, I have a chance to go to a better school, If I go to a better school, I get a chance of a better education, if I receive a better education, I have a chance to get a better job. I did all that and failed again, because the odds were against me as a young teenager. I hadn´t had the courage to say - "F" - you all; I am going to do and live what a BILLIONAIRE does in order to vibrate as a BILLIONAIRE. I did what broke people did. I had jobs and wasted money on stupid products / brands to impress my enemies. It took time until I realized I needed to change again. At the age of twenty four years young, eleven months after my birthday, I decided I can´t live LIFE like normal people anymore.

Sport and books have become my number one priority till this day. I am 42 years old these days (year 2021). Was it difficult? I tell you it is painful because your environment works on the frequency of being mediocre and broken. These people give up too easily. They prefer to blame everybody but themselves. I say all the time I am strong but definitely not a psychlogical strong hercules, there is a limit to how much pain I can accept. And that line has already been crossed that I will not appear publicly anymore.

Life is a journey of learning, growing and accepting. It is painful to accept reality as what it is.

You can shape your LIFE however you wish to shape your LIFE. All these insecure people who are calling you strange, or calling you stupid words such as you are ugly, fat, stupid, gay, transgender, nigger, bastard, fagot... etc, - what they do is point one finger at you. Technically, three other fingers are showing back to them. These people are insecure. They wanna be like you but they can´t. They wanna change their broken LIFE, but they are not willing to put consistent effort in it even if they don´t feel like it. My body has been well trained because I do sport at least three-hundred-fifty days a year. Even if I don´t feel like it I do sport.

The case is, nobody sees me doing sport. All they witness is the end RESULT of my sport exercises. The same with my books; nobody sees me texting or preparing a book. All they see is the finished book. Do you know how many people prefer to critique a book, but when you ask them, how many books have you written? The answer is: Not one single book.
See, whatever you do in LIFE, people will always find a way to keep you down. Imagine you could walk over water. Do you know how they're going to criticize you? He can walk over the water because he can't swim. See, the world is what it is. Instead of supporting you, you're going to deal with a lot of uninspirational set backs. You have the right to be whatever you wish to be in this world if you put the consistent effort into it.

Building a new paradigm / habitual behavior means you have to accept that you gonna fail at least one-hundred times. Do you know how tough it is to stop smoking if you are used to smoking two packages of cigarettes a day? The WANT to stop is there. But it does not happen overnight. It takes ninety to one-hundred days until you / your body / subconscious mind don´t have a need for a cigarette.

I created a billion dollar success company with my ordinary brain by changing my paradigm through consistent commitment. How many failures did I have to accept? I tell you: Over five thousand at least. Those failures are lessons for me. It dropped so deep into my

subconscious mindset that I am even afraid to get in touch with people who send the frequency of being strange. I just can't stand them anymore. I had to deal with these ignorant people when I was broke; I had to deal with them when I earned good money, I had to deal with them when I was broke again; I had to deal with them when I was a millionaire, and now I am on the frequency of a BILLIONAIRE. Why shall I deal with them again? What is the benefit. They don't help me to grow, they don't support my subconscious mindset; all they do is to try to keep me out of my vibration RESULT 0 BILLIONAIRE.

I came from nothing and I was so hungry to succeed that I wanted to master everything the best I could.

I started to do sport everyday; I started to read books every day; I gave up smoking cigarettes within twelve months; I developed a healthy attitude towards attracting the best money possible. What I needed to learn was to re-read books again and again. That came later in LIFE. I was so hungry for a better LIFE, that it was not an option to waste my LIFE in bars or discotheques. The change in my subconscious mind was a priority. Growth comes through pain. No pain no game.

You need to sacrifice if you wanna achieve something in LIFE. You wanna lose weight? Thus, sacrifice everything that keeps you fat and overweight. You have a broke financial mindset with zero RESULTS? Thus, sacrifice everything that keeps you with zero RESULTS.

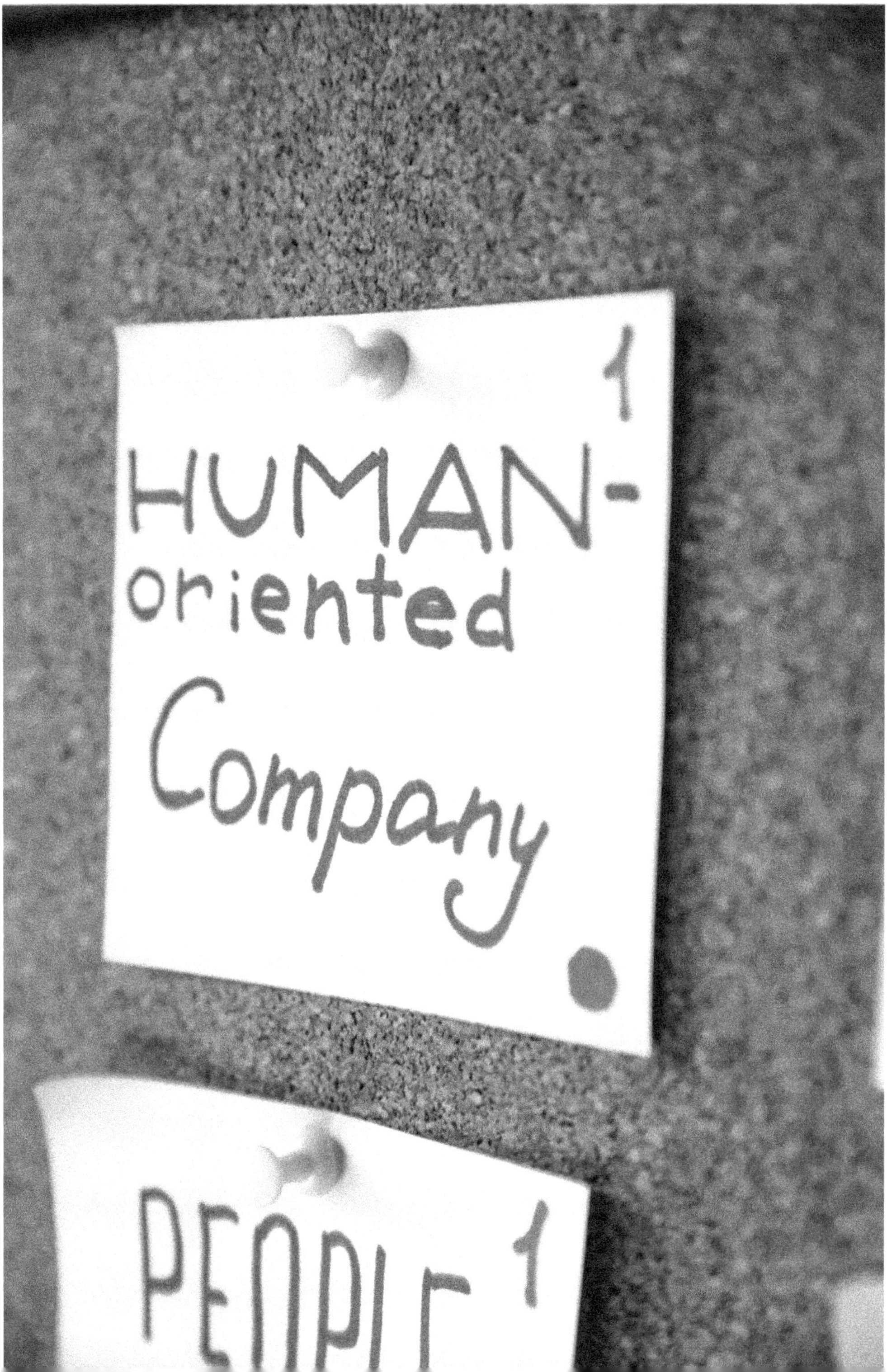
1
HUMAN-
oriented
Company
PEOPLE 1

How many classes have you ever attended to buy a business? How many classes have you ever had to sell a business? How many classes have you ever had in leadership? How many classes have you ever had in changing your subconscious mindset? How many classes have you ever had on how to invest money to earn billions?

See, the school system has been rotten. The world you are living in does not WANT you to RESULT as a BILLIONIARE. They WANT to keep you broke-minded on a rat wheel. You have to do everything for -SELF- if you WANT to vibrate like a BILLIONAIRE.

Remember, you are born rich and you have the right to live a LIFE full of richness. The only thing that is standing in your way is your poorly programed paradigm / habitual behaviour. Make it your habit to have a clean apartment. Make it your habit to read for at least two hours every day. Make it your habit to save as much money as you can.

———

If you keep working on your habit to become a BILIONAIRE you can´t help but to become a BILLIONAIRE. I tell you not to listen to you broke environment I urge you to buy books written by BILLIONAIRE.

I remember when I made $100 K a day, like as if it was yesterday. I was young, naive and wasted it. Yes, I wanted to impress all my enemies.

Why do those guys who changed the world have something in common? These strategic thinkers are tough as nails. They don't make excuses because they failed one or two times. They stand up and set their focus right. That is what I did after I wasted all my money. I went on my inside and figured out what it takes to be wealthy instead of being rich.

I should be ashamed of myself that I already had an idea of how to become a BILLIONAIRE but I was to weak to exercise everything that it takes to vibrate like a BILLIONAIRE.

Love won't get the work done. Action is the only possibility to go from A-B.

You can become a BILLIONAIRE like it is possible to fly to the moon. All you need is the WANT to do it. You can design your billion dollar success by setting up multiple sources of income. The amount of money you earn is in direct ratio to the need, for what you WANT to do to earn it, your ability to do it, and the difficulty there is in replacing you.

The need for what you do means: Does your idea serve billions of people? Steve Jobs invented the iPhone. It serves billions of people worldwide.

The ability to do it means: Are you working on your craft idea 24/7?

The difficulty replacing you means: Are you trusted by billions of people as a brand that they see a benefit in spending more money with you than with the competitor?

Earning money is competition. The best of the best end up being a BILLIONAIRE. It has nothing to do with being smart; it has something to do with how far you WANT to compete to succeed.

Imagine tennis player Serena Williams. There is a need for what she does, that's why she got all advertisment partners. She has the ability to remain among the best tennis players in the world. And she is very difficult to replace becuase she is a winner - she holds her position as the best tennis player in the world. The whole world is witnessing that it is difficult to compete against Serena Williams. She has multiple sources of income. She does not have another job; her main profession is being a tennis player.

If you are born poor it´s not your mistake, but if you die poor its your mistake.

Her passive income is in the advertising industry. Bill Gates and Warren Buffett say it simultaneously: BE FOCUS.

Minimize your regrets. You can't change your past. But you are in charge of what drops into your subconscious mindset. Change your future by studying the universal law of paradigm. Don´t care and waste your time what your environment thinks. Do you think Donald Trump gives a damn what you think about him? Do you think Bill Gates cares what you think of him? You are who you hang around with. Does your group look like a bunch of alpha lions?

If you don´t find a way to make money while you sleep, you will work until you die.

Surround yourself with those on the same mission as you. If your team does not look like a team of alpha lions, you waste your time. It means you gonna fail and can´t RESULT as a BILLIONAIRE. If you don´t WANT to RESULT as a BILLIONIARE like you need oxygen in your lungs, you hardly going to be qulified as a BILLIONAIRE.

You have to try to stay focused like a laser pointer. Bundle your energy to vibrate exclusively like a BILLIONAIRE.

You have to lose your broken DNA and exchange it for a new DNA of wealth.

Love does not bring you to RESULT as a BILIIONAIRE; religion does not transform you; sex does not bring you close to RESULT as a BILLIONAIRE. Nothing works but massive, consistent actions. You know what? Only one percent are going to RESULT as BILLIONAIRES.

Trust me, nobody gives a damn about you but YOU. Therefore, it is on - YOU - to change your future LIFE. If you fail one thousand times, the only person to blame is you, not your mother, father, or your stupid wife. You alone created the LIFE you are in. The LIFE you are in that broken circumstance is a reflection of your subconscious mindset. Your lack of knowledge is only consistent until you start to read and study and re-read and re-study consistently what you learned. Until it becomes a part of your paradigm / habitual behavior.

I know you WANT to fit in you WANT the world to like you. Remember what I said: Do you think the BILLIONAIRE DonaldTrump cares about other people opinion? Do you think Cornelius Vanderbilt cared about other people opinion? These people play the billion dollar game to succeed and not to feel sorry about the environment.Why? Because if they succeed, everybody is going to benefit from the billion dollar RESULT. I ask you again, why should you feel sorry if your stupid wife considers leaving you? Do you mean she WANTS to leave you because you are temporarily broke? I tell you, let that stupid wife go wherever she WANTS to go. All I urge you to do is not take her back if she shows up again.

Since that's impossible for the vast majority of us, I settled for inspiring BILLIONAIRE quotes. Maybe they don't give specifics, but perhaps they can point us in the right direction.

Take the situation as a man and hold your position as a man by the time she tries to re-connect with her so-called ex BILLIONAIRE husband. Your role model can't be your stupid ex-wife. Women are all over the place. What do these women bring to the table to support you during your journey to achieve the goal to becoem a BILLIONAIRE? Sex? Remember, sex gets not the work of a BILLIONAIRE done; LOVE brings you not closer to becoming a BILLIONAIRE. What you need is a massive paradigm transformation from being broke into a billion dollar RESULT.

Most of us are attracted to people where we fit in. Because we have a WANT to avoid the pain of rejection and growing. You grow up in an uncomfortable zone. Comfort is the killer of every success. Get comfortable being uncomfortable. And most financially broke people don't WANT that.

Subconsciously your brain will tell you any story why it´s not good to feel uncomfortable. It will always find an excuse why you shouldn't do that. Why? Because it is a mechanism to protect you from pain. Is it painful to be a leader? Let´s say, the transactional transformation you need to do to vibrate as a BILLIONAIRE you do it yourself completely alone. You earn your money alone and you're going to end up in a casket alone. A higher understanding of the financial game requires learning alone and to RESULT alone based on your understanding. You are, of course, not alone when people show up to criticize you. In the animal world, an eagle flies alone. That´s why he is called the king of the bird kingdom. Business is war; you are a warrior and are supposed to win the business battle. Once you become fearless, LIFE becomes limitless. What do you need critics for if they don´t wish to do better than you? Cut them out of your LIFE; you have been cast out of the LIFE of your former wife.

No matter how great your talent or efforts, some things just take time. You can´t produce a Baby in one month by getting nine women pregnant.

What you need as a future BILLIONAIRE is strictly the WANT to achieve your goal and leadership by mentors who have done it before. The rest are welcome to follow you as fans or welcome to stay away from you forever. It is lonely at the top. You wanna be everybody's friend? Stay mediocre and apply for a nine-to-five job. Warren Buffett has only one best friend and that is Charlie Munger. They share a friendship for over seventy years. How many friends do you really need? Of course he shares a good connection with Bill Gates, but Mister Gates is not his friend. Steve Jobs had no friends. Michael Jackson had one female friend that used to be Liz Taylor. They got along because they understood what it meant to be a child star. If you have more than five friends ask them to invite you for a drink. If they refuse, cut them off. Of course you invited them more than twenty times. That is what I do all the time. They want me to get a free meal? They must be out of their mind if they think I gonna do it until I die. Ray Kroc had no friends. Money doesn't buy you friends. Those friends who are around me are with me since I started as a broke man. We share such a strong bond for each other that it does not matter if I might go broke tomorrow, ok? If you got a gold digger bitch as a sex object, all I can say: She knows the game and you understand what you put yourself into. Has she got old? Of course you replace her ass with a younger version. You go broke, and she replaces you with another ugly-looking guy. That is your game, none of my business. Do you think Melania Trump does not understand the game with an ugly-looking Donald Trump? Of course she does. If he runs out of money, guess what the deal is. See, you are not here to complain about LIFE.

How much sacrifice are you willing to make to achieve your billion dollar goal? Everything is possible. Just step on the frequency of a BILLIONAIRE and start vibrating like a BILLIONAIRE that you have the chance to RESULT as a BILLIONAIRE.

Success is the greatest middle finger of all time.

Go deep inside of you and start to hate the old you that keeps you away from a succesful LIFE as a BILLIONAIRE. This guy is not worthy of living in your subconscious mind. Cut that nobody systematically out of your paradigm / habitual behavior. The truth hurts. And it's painful to accept the truth. But the real pain comes from stepping consistently on the frequency of change till the day you're gonna die. Life is a competition; business is a competition; success is a competition. If you hate to compete, don´t even dare to dream of becoming a BILLIONAIRE.

I care only about one thing in LIFE, and that is to serve something higher. Because I do it, I automatically RESULT till this day as a BILLIONAIRE. I have a dream to succeed till the day I die. I used to work as a waiter. I did work behind a DJ desk; I did garden work; I did work as a pizza deliverer; I used to serve alcohol behind a bar; I used to clean floors; I used to work as a call center agent. I did all kinds of jobs. You can bet I am well experienced in LIFE. But the real benefit came when I became an independent thinker. Think and Grow Rich by Napoleon Hill became my number one medicine for my successful subconscious mindset. Everything I am today I owe it to Napoleon Hill.

Your life is boring because you have boring friends.

Steve Jobs
1955 - 2011

The ones who are crazy enough to think that they can change the world, are the ones who do.

Do the things other will not do.

Steve Jobs:
"The only way to do great work is to love what you do. If you have not found it yet, keep looking. Don´t settle. As with all matters of the heart, you´ll know when you find it."

If you want to be strong learn to fight alone

Ten years from now I want to be able to look back and say, damn I am glad I hustled

Success can´t happen without going through some of your hardest sacrifices.

Take the risk or lose the chance

Success is the greatest middle finger of all time.

I don´t have dreams I have goals to achieve.

Never depend on one single income. Make an investment to create a second source.

Do not put the eggs in one basket.

Sacrifice few years of partying for decades of freedom.

Either I will find a way or create a way but I will not create an excuse.

Real is rare and fake is everywhere.

Friends will leave you until you become successful.

If you want to send your child to a better school, you need more money, If you WANT to have a better car, If you wish to invite a woman to a better restaurant, it all takes money and not zen. The taxi driver does not take zen as a currency, nor does the landlord. These people wish to see cash as liquid money. Most of us walk through life with the emergency brakes on. Then they release what happens? Yes, the car is not easy to control. The same apply in real LIFE. I guarantee if you finish the book and start to re-read it again, your goals are going to be at least eight-hundred times bigger, because you understand that a paradigm shift is required to RESULT as a BILLIONAIRE.

Sensitivity equals poverty? Only if you don´t know how to use that godly given talent.

ONCE YOU BECOME FEARLESS LIFE BECOMES LIMITLESS

I am obsessed will building my emipirer

Trust me they gonna ignore you until they realize how successful you are.

Stay original and let the world copy you.

Imagine you have no fear regarding the outside world. The only thing you carry to the grave are regrets in the sense of I should have done this or that.

LIFE is all about consistent change. You have to put your foot on the gas. Go to the next level of learning, serving, and earning. Because you always attract what you are in harmony with. You have to be in harmony with a higher level of service for your customers if you wish them to spend more money on you. Imagine you are operating at the best version of yourself every day; that is your intention; you are going to attract what is available on that higher frequency with that standard. Your environment is going to change because the new environment fits the new level of standard. You gonna surround yourself with how you wanna live. If we are not operating at a higher level of a new standard, that´s where contemptment and setteling comes in.

I am so tired of not being a BILLIONAIRE.

Only a king can attract a queen and only a queen can keep a king focused.

Hustle until your haters start asking for a job.

You are now in control of the transmission to form your subconscious mindset into the behavior of a BILLIONAIRE. There is a real enemy you are dealing with.

One that is strategizing against you, holding you tightly bound to the comfort of your current RESULTS. This enemy is restless and scheming against you. Attacking your emotions and coming after your mind, your body, your relationships, and your future.

Conquer your new BILLIONAIRE paradigm like you go to war. It is your future, your money, your time that should exclusively RESULT in a billion dollar success. Upgrade your LIFE by studying the law of a BILLIONAIRE. Don´t allow your old paradigm to control your successful future. Don´t let the present RESULTS control your future actions. A paradigm changes through consistent repetition. You repeat reading this book one-hundred times, and you can't help but change your habitual behaviour.

If your subconscious mind is in order, everything will follow. Your attitude to studying what changes your paradigm is the first step into a billion dollar dream. The impact is going to be hugh. Once you start observing your beheaviour, you must go very deep, but you can´t help but to win a new subconscious mindset. No idea works until you change your subconscious mindset.

The only thing people are missing is the right direction. Learn from someone who already done this.

Discipline is the key to financial freedom. You have to discipline your thinking. If you control your thinking, your actions towards your goals are going to change.

Remember, complexity is the enemy of success. It does not take twenty years to change your paradigm. As I told you before, the WANT to do it is important. You WANT to quit smoking? It takes approximately three to six months to quit smoking, eventually twelve months if you are a heavy smoker. But it can´t take twenty years. The same with the subconscious mindset, it takes discipline to WANT it.

You can´t build a reputation on what you are going to do.

the big paradigm change. It does not take twenty years. The discipline gives you a time gap of three months to twelve months where you are in total control to build a sustainable business. Is it going to be easy? Well, ask any smoker in the world if it was easy to quit smoking, ask any former overweight man / woman in the world, if it was easy to lose weight. Yes, it´s a challenge to be full of discipline 24/7 three-hundred-sixty-five days a year. You know what: It's worth it.

Your daily ritual creates your subconscious mindset. Let me tell you something: Remember when you went to school, remember when the teacher tried to teach you 6X7 = 42 - remember how difficult it was to retain that information. You know what it took to remember it? Consistent repetition. The same with a BILLIONAIRE habitual behavior that can´t help, but attract billions of dollars, it requires consistent repetition until it becomes a part of your subconscious DNA. Do the work and start the shift of your paradigm. As I told you before, you have to repeat reading this book at least one-thousand times until it becomes a part of your subconscious mind. If it´s in your subconscious mindset your habitual behavior can´t help but attract billions of dollars. Is it easy? I leave the interpretation this time up to you.

Everything starts with an SELF image. People their present RESULT control them, so it affects their SELF esteem.

A lot of people don't have a good understanding of money. Because we have been taught to ignore every single fact when it comes to money. We have never been taught during our school time how to function to attract billions of money. Because our teachers were not programed to think like BILLIONIARE. Money is an attitude; multiple-sources of income is an attitude, to have a good body shape is an attitude; living in a clean apartment is an attitude.

If you ask one-hundred people what they WANT ninety-five to ninety-seven don´t know what they WANT exactly; they rather tell you what they don't WANT. Imagine if we shifted that and focused on what we really WANT, the WANT should be first a new subconscious mindset. How do we do one thing is how we do everything. It´s not that we can´t have what we WANT; we have to discipline our subconscious mindset through our mind by disciplining what we put in our mind. Everything comes with our thinking.

Don´t allow small minds convince you that your dreams are too big.

And as we get emotionally involved in it, then you're gonna see the fruits of your labour. Your mind is a garden. Whatever seed you plant, you're gonna earn that back. That's what you have to do as a future BILLIONAIRE, you have to plant the BILLIONAIRE seed in your mind, that it drops down into your subconscious mindset, that it becomes your habitual behavior to act as a BILLIONAIRE who can't help but attract billions of dollars. How to do it? I gonna repeat: Step on the frequency of a BILLIONAIRE by reading and re-reading and re-studying the law of a BILLIONAIRE as if you were a professional athlete like Kobe Bryant, LeBron James, Michael Jordan, or Cristiano Ronaldo. Be obsessed to shift your paradigm from being broke and uneducated into a behavior of a BILLIONAIRE. Whatever you want in LIFE, you have to plant it into the garden of your mindset. The mind takes everything you you give it. It can't reject what you give it. It then drops into your subconscious mindset and your body does what your subconscious mindset has been programed to do.

If you plant one-thousand book readings into your mind, it drops sooner or later into your subconscious mindset, then you see opportunities to make billions and your body acts to accumulate billions of dollars. Why? Because you planted the BILLIONAIRE seed into your subconscious mindset. All information is available in your paradigm to react as a BILLIONAIRE who can't help but attract billions of dollars. If you are not discipline with your mind and see it as a valuable field where you are in charge to plant the right information necessary, the right informations can only be books written by BILLIONAIRES, seminars given by BILLIONAIRES, YOUTUBE video by BILLIONAIRES, that is the only seed that is worth entering your field / mind / subconscious mindset, don't wonder if you can't RESULT as a BILLIONAIRE if you are not willing to work the field / mind / subconscious mindset.

If you do exactly as I told you, your LIFE can only transform into a billion dollar success.

Most people want to know what to do to RESULT as a BILLIONAIRE. The case is you need to learn to think like a BILLIONAIRE if you WANT to RESULT as a BILLIONAIRE. You can't RESULT as a BILLIONAIRE if you don't have the subconscious mindset to think like a BILLIONAIRE. If you can't think like a BILLIONAIRE you can't see all those opportunities to make billions of dollars.

It´s ok if you don´t like me not everyone has a good taste.

Remember, the idea is already in your mind to attract billions of dollars. Kennedy had already had the idea to fly to the moon. The WANT to do it was also already there. The next step was to take massive effort and consistent actions to fly to the moon. The same apply to your BILLIONAIRE dream. It requires conscious actions to make it a reality on planet Earth. If you have an idea in your mind, all you need to do is program your subconscious mindset so that your body can step into action to collect billions of dollars. If your subconscious mind has been programed to think like a BILLIONAIRE, all you have to do is accept the idea that an opportunity is there. If your subconscious mindset tells you something, just do it. Because it gives you leadership where the money is hidden.

For you to win as a BILLIONAIRE you have to work your subconscious mindset like a farmer works his field to plant seeds.
If you do exactly what is written in the book, you gonna RESULT as a BILLIONAIRE. I know that for a fact.

If you allow yourself to focus on your current circumstances, we are creating the same RESULTS in the future. This book teaches you how not to allow your current RESULTS to control you, how to really discipline yourself, and how to create what you WANT.

If you WANT to live like the top three percent, you have to think like those people at the top, you have to act like those top people, you have to be it, right now. If you are like them immediately, you gonna RESULT within twelve months into their subconscious mindset. How serious are you about making the change instantly? Are sick and tired of being sick and tired and financially broke? Do everything that brings you to the future LIFE of a BILLIONAIRE. Your current way does not work because you are obviously broke and overweight. It you do what is written in this book for exactly one year, you are going to have a completely different LIFE. If you don't repeat to re-study this book again, you gonna be living the same way.
You are currently facing a lot of pressure because the RESULTS are not good enough to pay all your bills. I ask you again: What do you have to lose if you try my way?

You will never reach your goal if you stop and throw stones at every dog that barks.

There is a difference between being interested in creating the LIFE you WANT and being committed. When we are interested we do what is convenient; when we are committed we do whatever it takes to RESULT; we don´t accept excuses. It ´s not to do it some of the time when it´s convinient; it´s to do whatever it takes to RESULT as a BILLIONAIRE. If you are holding your resistance in you, you are not allowing your true potential / greatness to come out. Go that extra mile every day until you die, do that extra action, you gonna be shocked how effective your RESULTS sre gonna be.

Every next level of your life will demand a different you.

The best way to become a BILLIONAIRE is to help one-billion people.

Be somebody nobody thought you could be.

If you are not in harmony with the frequency of money, you are never gonna attract billions of dollars. You only attract what you are in harmony with. Your apartment is a dirty mess; it means you are in harmony to live like that. If your clothes are dirty, it means you are in harmony with your dirty clothes. You are financially broke; it means you are in harmony with almost no money. Your current RESULTS are the attraction of what you are in harmony with. These are absolute universal laws. The question is how much is enough.

You are the highest and most perfect creation by The Lord. You are on planet earth to have a wonderful descent-rich LIFE. If you are overweight and live in a dirty mess-up apartment, you should consider the fact that there is something wrong with your paradigm. If you are additionally broke, there is definitely something wrong with your habitual behavior. Let go of your old habitual behavior and step into a new zone full of discipline.

Are you attracted to a new BILLIONAIRE LIFE? Attraction is another universal law. Expectation evokes the law of attraction. Expectations trigger the law of attraction. Expectation is a mindset. The next step is vibration. Everything in this world vibrates. Everything moves nothing rests. Growing is vibrations. If you change from being broke to a BILLIONAIRE, you vibrate into something where you have never been.

Stop being ignorant, and step into the opposite, which is knowledge and wisdom. Because you are in an ignorant state, you will worry and be full of doubts. The polar opposite of worry and doubt is UNDERSTANDING. From understanding you develop into the state of FAITH. The only possibility to develop UNDERSTANDING is through consistent STUDY. Fear manifests as anxiety and FAITH means WELL BEING.

The Fear: Whenever you do something you have never done before, it´s gonna be natural that you gonna expirience the FEAR. The unknown causes the FEAR. If you understand the creative process, remember you are a creative being, then you can manage to walk around the FEAR.

Let me explain how the mind works. On the conscious LEVEL we have a choice. We can stay ignorant or on the opposite if we study, we can develop understanding. Thus, if you study and re-study this book, you can have anything you WANT in your LIFE.

Success does not come and find you, you have to step out and get it.

You have to make a choice. Do you WANT to stay ignorant and financially broke as you are, or do you want to step on the opposite of being ignorant and shift into a mind of UNDERSTANDING. The choice is up to you. You can change your habitual behavior that gives you billions of dollars.

No one is coming to save you. This LIFE is 100% your responsibility.

Work until you no longer have to introduce yourself.

Don´t stress what you cannot chance.

The richest people in the world build networks; everyone else is trained to look for work.

Take the risk. If you win you will be happy. If you lose you gonna be wiser.

Henry Ford

If I had asked people what they wanted, they would had said: "Faster horses..."

The futture is all yours.

Innovation is saying no to 1,000 things.

It´s not about how many times you fall, but how many times you get back.

Discipline allows you to build yourself sustainably.

People overestimate what they can do in a year and underestimate what they can do in 10 years.

The smallest progress is still progress.

The closer you are to money, the higher the chances you´ll get some of it.

Dept is just a more sophisticated form of slavery.

If you want to win, you can´t let the slow runners dictate your rhythm.

1. Get your money to work

2. Change your subconscious mindset to RESULT as a BILLIONAIRE

3. Have a strong WANT

4. Hate your current unaesthetic life

5. Never forget how much effort it took to make the first airplane fly

6. Commit fully

7. Collaborate

8. Change your surroundings

9. Be on a mission

10. Help at least one billion people